Who stole my identity?

Who stole my identity?

Ángel Martínez

Who stole my identity?

Story based on true events

Who stole my identity?

Who stole my identity?

THANKS

I wish to express my gratitude to the people who have given me their support in moments of solitary experience and hours of introspection, as it is for me to write a book, when we are accompanied by the thought that follows the plot and that loneliness that is only understood by those who write the story that is part of our own life.

I make a count and the names of countless friends and colleagues come to my mind to whom I wish to give the recognition they deserve, but sometimes there are so many that, just by naming each one of them, they would fill several pages, in this edition I limit myself to quoting only some of those who were and will be friends for eternity for one reason or another:

Aivan Martínez: My son who showed me the importance of Love.

Ismail C: Special Agent "FBI" A Man of Law.

Mark F.: Special Agent "FBI", my friend.

Bijan Parwaresch: Former U.S. Attorney, now Federal Attorney.

Ashley: You taught me the value of a smile.

Ismael Martínez: Who went to war to live and see hell in real time.

And finally, to my unconditional editor Gladys Montes, who made the materialization of this work possible.

"A man's freedom is measured by the ability he has to take responsibility for the consequences of his actions".

Anonymous

Who stole my identity?

INTRODUCTION

In an increasingly interconnected world, personal identity has become one of the most valuable and, at the same time, vulnerable assets. The book "Who Stole My Identity?" demonstrates with a real case that occurred 20 years ago that this topic is still relevant and that, with technological advances, the complexities of identity theft have multiplied. This crime not only threatens our financial security, but also our personal integrity.

The first edition published in Spanish: ¿Quién se ha robado mi identidad? Ten years ago, when Facebook was beginning to change the way it interacts with social networks, was a success.

Every day we witness many cases of identity theft, we see and read about it in the media and social networks, which is why after all these years, especially after the pandemic in 2020, my editor and friend Gladys Montes has encouraged me to republish the work and update the alarming data on the subject.

This book not only describes with real facts how criminals can appropriate our identity, but also provides information to protect us against this growing danger. As we delve into this reading, we will not only discover a shocking true story, but it also invites you to reflect on how to prevent and combat this crime in our daily lives.

Millions of users are victims of identity theft every year. With the accelerated shift to digital banking, many more are likely to experience some form of identity theft soon, if they haven't already.

Identity theft in the digital world today is very different than it was a decade ago. In the past, consumers knew they were victims if a creditor called them asking, for example, about a bad check. But now, with the rise in data breaches exposing sensitive personal information and the use of synthetic identities, consumers need to be more proactive to avoid being the next victims.

With the shift in consumer habits post-pandemic, it's essential for everyone to understand how to stay safe from scammers who take advantage of a stolen identity to commit scams, fraud, and theft.

"Who Stole My Identity?" is essential reading to understand the importance of protecting our identity in an ever-evolving digital world.

I hope that this reading is useful and that you share it with your loved ones and friends.

Remember, it is in your hands to protect yourself. Any foresight is little.

1

A GREAT PLAN

Two men left the room of the modest hotel located in Downtown Miami, to enter the branch of the bank that was four blocks away from the place where they had prepared the operation: robbing a bank in broad daylight. The costume was almost perfect, identical to the photo on Facebook, from which the data had been taken to create the criminal who would leave the traces. They prepared a perfect alibi that would allow them to remain within organized crime, without anyone suspecting them.

To create the IDs and get the credit cards ready, they got the complete date of birth that Dante Antonio Hank had on his profile on the popular social network Facebook. With a little makeup and a wig, the same color as his hair, the assailant was sure that the bank tellers would identify him as soon as the police began the investigations into the case.

The assailants knew exactly what to do; they were carrying two strong plastic bags and once inside the bank branch, they asked two of the tellers to put all the money they had in their possession in them; Previously, the cashiers were warned that, if they made the mistake of doing something different from what they requested, they would be killed by shots that would pierce their bodies in fractions of seconds.

The two young employees of the Bank, who were duly trained to act naturally in these cases, acted immediately, following the instructions of the robbers to the letter, giving them the sum of $1,300,000, a considerable amount that completely fulfilled the expectations of the assailants.

The criminals left the bank carrying their loot, without worrying that the cameras would capture it since they knew perfectly well that their disguise protected them from any future persecution, in case they were not caught on the spot.

Carrying bags full of money, they went to a car where a third subject was waiting ready to start the car that he kept with the engine running to leave the parking lot. They left slowly, knowing that the license plate or identification of the car they were driving would be captured by the cameras that protected the building.
The intruders were out of sight when they heard the sirens of the police patrol cars, who, alerted by the bank's alarm system, were approaching the scene of the robbery. Colored lights and bulletproof vests were present; the scene area was sealed off to be handled by FBI experts.

The thieves left the car abandoned, changed their clothes, took another car and disappeared without leaving the slightest trace of who they really were. All that remained was to complete what would be the great evidence. The men parked near the other bank located about twenty kilometers away from where the robbery was carried out, they said goodbye to the man who would serve as a decoy so that he could continue with his next move.

He took out a wad of bills that he had prepared with $4,000.00, entered the bank with the same disguise used in the robbery committed minutes before and deposited the money in an account that would later be associated with the license plate of the car that had been abandoned. Once this transaction was completed, he went to a branch of Western Union, to credit the sum of $3,000.00 to a prepaid card. He stared at the camera, letting it take him full length, once again, he was making the work easier for the FBI agents. After this activity was completed, the thief disappeared leaving enough evidence to never be caught and his theft to become a perfect crime.

"Sad time ours! It is easier to disintegrate an atom than a prejudice."

Albert Einstein

2

IT'S A CONSPIRACY

I began to fall asleep due to fatigue; I felt exhausted from the excessive activity of the previous day. It was 2:00 a.m. when the phone on the bedside table on the right side of my bed began ringing. I thought I was dreaming, but when I woke up completely, I realized that someone required my services or that some prankster had gone too far and wanted to end his night with a conversation with the private detective "me", who would surely be sleeping.

I picked up the phone to see what it was and try to sleep again; I needed a few hours of sleep to regain the necessary strength so that my fragile body, the next day, as usual, could get up and engage in some activities that required my personal attention.
-Hello
-Who's speaking?
- Who did you call?
-I am interested in talking to the private detective or the writer who is the same person.
- Who calls him?
-My name is Dante Hank.
-Ángel Martínez, how can I help you?
-I know that this time is not the most appropriate time to call you, but I need you to understand me, my only son is in prison without any possibility of being released.
- What happened to your child?
-The story is long, my friend.
- Who gave you my phone number?

-At the moment I am finishing reading one of your books and I am fully convinced that you are the man I need.
- Could this matter wait until tomorrow?
-I'm sorry, Mr. Martinez, I can't sleep; It's about my son.
-Okay, I'll sleep another time, let me get up; Wait a moment please.
-Okay, I'll stay online until I get back on the phone."

A situation like this occurs daily in the life of a private detective; we do not have a schedule that allows us to lead a normal lifestyle like that of any ordinary citizen.

Duty called me and I had to forget that my body was crying out to let it rest for a few more hours. I got out of bed and in the company of my faithful friend Spike, "my dog", we went in the direction of the kitchen to start an old electric coffee maker that did everything, when I almost had the coffee ready, I said:
-Mister Dante
-Yes.
- What book are you reading?
-Finished reading Operation Hook.
-That was an extraordinary adventure.
-You are as I imagined.
- What do you think I'm like?
-If someone calls me at 2:00 in the morning, when I am trying to sleep, after an exhausting day, as I am sure you have had, I will send you straight to the devil, however, you are treating me as if we were friends from many years ago; He has taken the time to talk to this desperate old man who can't sleep.
-Don't trust that behind my kind attention there is a dollar sign, ha, ha, ha.
-When they treat me well, I like to pay the cost regardless of the amount. I think we will understand each other for sure.
- Ha, ha, ha, you have a sense of humor.
-That is fate, Mr. Dante.
- I don't believe in that shit!
-Nothing happens by chance in this life; I believe that everything that happens has a reason for being.

-You are a man with many experiences, you will have to say it for a reason, but I only believe in what I see.
-Now I want you to tell me what's going on with your son, I don't want to bore him with my beliefs.
-My boy has almost the same name as me, the difference is that his name is Dante Antonio Hank.
-I want you to start by telling me in what prison they are being held.
-It's at the Federal Detention Center in Miami.
- What are you accused of?
-Of robbing a bank.
- Robbery of several banks or one in particular?
-They accuse you of robbing one of the branches of the Bank of America.
- Have you talked to your child?
-Yes, the problem is that my son can lie to everyone, but I assure you that he would never lie to his father.
"This makes me think that your son assures you that he is innocent.
"Yes, I want to hire you to find out who is really to blame for that theft."
- Do you have an attorney in this case?
-No
"What you mean is that the court assigned you a public one."
-Correct.
-I need your son's general information and please give me an account of what happened; Then I'll see what the feds say in the indictment report.

This was the beginning of the investigation of a case where only the victim's father had hope, as he fully trusted the version given to him by his son, on whom a terrible accusation weighed. All the evidence in his arrest report convicted him.

Having from experience that the people detained, in 99.9% of the cases, say they are innocent, and it is a guarantee of the law:

"Everyone is innocent until proven guilty"

"Innocent is he who does not need to explain himself".

Albert Camus

3

THE THIRD EYE

On August 7, 2009, Friday at 9:00 a.m., the cameras of a branch of the Bank of America recorded photos of two men standing in front of tellers 4 and 5, passing him a note announcing an assault and demanding that they hand over all the money they had in their boxes.

The photos showed a young man dressed in a red shirt, who protected his face with glasses, he was very similar to the son of Mr. Dante Hank. When the robbers left the bank with the loot, the parking lot cameras captured a red Ford Taurus car, identification plate number XT6-93N that after being found abandoned in a park near the bank branch that was robbed, it was proven that it was owned by the young Dante Antonio Hank.

Inside the car a photo of the owner wearing the shirt he was wearing when the robbery was committed was found, said photo had been taken in front of the house located at the address where the statements of a Visa card, prepaid, arrived, to which half an hour after the robbery $3,000.00 were deposited and the statements of a checking account in the name of the accused, in which, 45 minutes after the robbery, $4,000.00 were deposited. The images captured by the cameras of the bank where the deposit was made coincided with the person who carried out the robbery in box 4 of Bank of America, who had been identified as Dante Antonio Hank.

With this evidence, the feds had the case solved; the young Hank, had been found guilty of the robbery along with two accomplices still unknown.
As before, I had seen the devil turned into God, I said that desperate father.
-I will visit your son in prison.
- Will you take my case?
-After I visit him, we'll talk.

Knowing that the FBI has all the resources of the United States government, I had to find clues that would convince me that it was worth initiating a counter-investigation of this nature. He had to be sure that we could prove that the defendant was innocent of the charges against him so as not to waste the time and hopes that this young man's father had.

I immediately got all the reports that the FBI had on the case, I went to the center of the city, where the Federal Prison of Miami, Florida is.
After completing all the paperwork that is required of private investigators when visiting a detainee inside a federal prison in the United States, I requested that I be allowed in to interview Mr. Hank's son.

In this case there were two things to weigh:
a) The father who was convinced of his son's innocence.
b) The accused had to say that he was innocent as many people do when they are arrested.

With morale on the floor, due to the facts documented in the FBI indictment, I entered the prison compound to speak with Mr. Hank's son.

I sat in one of the glass-walled rooms were lawyers and detectives interview defendants. As I waited, I thought about those young people whose lives have been paralyzed by being deprived of their liberty in a country where there is the largest prison population in the world, which is about 8.3 million people, counting those who are on probation, "with electronic shackles" to be monitored in their homes or workplaces. The politicians of the United

States are so brazen that even with this embarrassment of being the number one drug users in the world, they are the ones who certify those who are doing the job of fighting organized crime well, but I ask myself, who certifies the United States?

We will leave politics for another book, now we will continue with the story of the arrested young man. My client's son appeared through the door that leads to the main corridor of the prison, after having undergone a routine search, which consists of pulling down his pants to insert a finger into his anus in some checks; This search is carried out on the inmates every time they leave or enter their cells, to prevent them from taking out or entering any object inside their bodies. Some prisoners prefer not to visit him so as not to undergo these uncomfortable anal examinations.

When the young man entered the room where I was, I was struck by the fragility of his body.

-My name is Angel Martinez, I'm a private detective, your father, Mr. Dante Hank, wants me to look at the evidence that the FBI has against you.
-Thank you very much for coming.
-We will try to see what is happening with your case.
-I don't know where all this mess comes from, I assure you, Mr. Martinez, that this is a great conspiracy.
-That's why I came to visit you, we will do an analysis to see if it is worth initiating a counter-investigation into his case.
- Where do we start?

I had the young man where I wanted him, interested in my work; This is the first thing a good researcher does when they visit the prospect for the first time.

People who are imprisoned sometimes get upset, block themselves and refuse to accept what happened and shout from the rooftops that they are innocent.

In my long career as a researcher, I have had experiences with clients who in my presence see a video or photos where they appear and categorically deny that these are them.

I took a notebook from my portfolio to make notes that I would later analyze with my young prospect, who was desperate when he saw my slow movements, like any caged beast, he attacked me with the following question:

- Mr. Martinez, do you believe in my innocence?
-Don't worry, Dante Antonio, take this easy, after all, at the moment you have nowhere to go.
-You did not answer my question, Mr. Martinez.
-The arrest documents say that you are guilty; I'm here to do an analysis and see if there are any indications that this is a conspiracy.
-You still don't answer what I asked.
-To answer your question, I will tell you the following: If I take away what I have seen, you are guilty; Now, I want to hear your side of the story to compare it with the data that I have and then we talk.
-I agree.
-Very well, it is very important that we understand each other.

The young man wanted to gauge my ability and see if I was true research professional or if he just wanted his father's money. I didn't tell him what he wanted to hear and just looked at the evidence I had gotten.
The channel of communication had been opened and we understood each other easily; He realized that, if he did not find a path to travel, I would withdraw from the investigation without wasting his father's time or money.

Who stole my identity?

I continued with my interrogation:

-Let's talk about how you start your activities on any given day.

-I am studying finance at FIU, (Florida International University)

- What are the days and times of your classes?

-I get up from Monday to Friday at 5:00 in the morning, I leave for the University at about 7:00 in the morning and I take my first class at 8:00 every morning. I only have Saturdays and Sundays off.

- What time do you return home?

-I spend all day on campus, I leave at 5:00 in the afternoon and when I get home, I take a bath, eat something and review any homework I have pending.

- Do you do the same routine every week?

-Yes

- Do you have a girlfriend?

-I met a young woman on Facebook, but nothing serious.

-Let's talk about the evidence

-They say that you went to the bank at 9:00 in the morning to commit a robbery and then you went to another bank to deposit $4,000.00 in your checking account.

-I never left the University.

- Do you have someone who can testify that they were with you between 9:00 and 10:00 a.m.?

-I was reading in the courtyard of the University for about two hours on a topic that I had to present at noon.

- Don't have an alibi?

-No, sir.

So far, I had not found anything that indicated that my possible client was not the one who carried out the robbery of the Bank.

-Let's talk about your car, the red Ford Taurus.

-I'm very confused, I don't understand how it is possible that my car was found abandoned in a park.

Who stole my identity?

- Where did you park it when you arrived at the University?

-I stopped for a moment to talk to the guard at the entrance to the university campus, it was 8:00 in the morning, he says that at about 8:30 that morning I left his door again driving my car. That can't be true, Mr. Martinez, hu, hu, hu.

-Don't worry, my friend, it's not the time to cry; If you're innocent I'll find out, that's what I'm here for.

-Excuse me, sir, I feel helpless; I am innocent, and all the evidence accuses me. I can't resist it!

-Can you swear to me that the one who was driving your car at 8:30 in the morning, was not you?

-I swear to God, Mr. Martinez.

-How many keys does your car have?

-Two.

-Where did you leave the other key?

-My father keeps it in his safe.

-Is it possible that someone has taken that key?"

-Impossible, the key is in the safe and my father is the only person who has the combination.

-Did you know that your car appeared without any damage? That is why we believe that whoever handled it had a key.

-That is not possible, sir.

-How long do you have with that car?

-My father bought it about three months ago.

The young man gave me no clue, the deeper I went into my interrogation, the more guilty he seemed.

-This is very important

-Tell me.

-Try to make a count from the day your father gave you the car until the day of the theft; It's very important that you remember every moment that is related to your car.

-The first week I tinted its windows.

-What happened next?

-I don't remember anything important.

-Have you ever lent the car to a friend, a family member or your girlfriend?

-Yes.

-Who did you lend it to?

-I remember that a neighbor asked me to borrow it to go to the supermarket since the tow truck had taken his because it was broken.

-What is that man's name?

-My father calls him Diego.

-When did that happen?

-About three weeks ago.

-What day of the week was it when you lent Mr. Diego the car?

-One Saturday morning, we saw that a tow truck was loading his vehicle; He came over to where I was with my father to ask if we could lend him my car for fifteen minutes to go to the supermarket.

-How long has that man been your neighbor?

-You moved into that house about four months ago.

-Does your father have a car?

-Yes.

-When Diego made his request, were the two cars parked in front of your house?

-Yes.

-Do you remember his words exactly?

-Mr. Diego said: Mr. Hank, can you lend me your son's car for about 15 minutes to go to the supermarket that is 5 blocks from here?

-What did your father answer?

-With pleasure. Then we gave him the key.

-What happened next?

Who stole my identity?

-Half an hour later, Mr. Diego brought us a bottle of wine as a thank you gift.

I had finally found an interesting clue! I could already begin to inquire about abnormal things, because until now I had felt cornered without knowing where to get into the game. The conspiracy, if there was one, was covering every point where an investigator could enter.

-Tell me about your girlfriend, how did you meet her?

-Through Facebook.

-Who invited whom?

-I'm not very sociable, but one day I went to my page and found an invitation from a beautiful woman.

-What happened next?

-I accepted her as a friend.

-What is her name?

-Her name is Carmen.

-Was there any meeting?

-We wrote to each other until one day we decided to meet.

-When was the first time you met that woman?

-Approximately five months ago.

-Where did you meet?

-Mr. Martinez, I think you are deviating from what really matters.

-I don't think so.

-What does my private life have to do with the accusation of theft that they are making against me?

-Let me tell you something young man, the only thing you can count on is your father who believes in you no matter what they say or what appears against you; He wants to hire me and I'm trying to find a needle in a haystack. I'll give you some advice, right now you're at the gate of hell and you have in front of you the only person who can help you.

-I don't want her to get angry, but I think Carmen has nothing to do with this.

-Well, you think wrong, everything is important here, and if you want my help you will have to trust my experience, or else I will be forced to leave your case.

I had to put him in his place because I noticed that he was behaving like the prisoners; They think they know everything, they think they are very intelligent, but sometimes they talk nonsense.

-Let us continue, Mr. Martinez.
-Where did you meet Carmen?
-I went to visit her at her house.
-What happened?
-Carmen, was very excited.
-Who opened the door of their house for you?
-Herself.
-Does she live alone?
-Yes.
-What is her last name?
-I don't remember, but she told me.
-What happened when she opened the door?
-She came out and gave me a hug.
-Did she kiss you?
-Not at that time.
-Was she shy or expressive?
-She said that that moment was wonderful and that it had to be captured.
-Capture it how?
-She came out with a camera so that we could take a picture.
-Did you take the photo?
-A man was passing by the place and Carmen asked him to take our photo.
-Did you take them?
-Yes, we left smiling.
-How was she dressed?

-She had a yellow dress above the knees, she looked divine.

-You, what clothes were you wearing?

-A red shirt and jeans.

-How many photos were taken?

-Just one.

-Do you both appear in that photo?

-Yes.

-Why did this photo appear in your car?

I looked for the file that I had next to me next to my briefcase and I took a copy of the photo that was taken of the young man on the same day of the meeting with the charming Carmen, without him noticing. She looked smiling in front of the address that he later confirmed to me was that of his girlfriend.

-Where did that photo come from?

-It's you?

-Yes, and that's her house.

-You tell me, because that photograph was in your car, the FBI has it as evidence.

-I don't remember when I took that photo.

-If you notice, this photograph was taken by a third person since it shows one side of the body of your lovely lady.

-I told you that she asked a stranger for the favor.

-I don't believe that story.

-You mean to tell me that she was composed with someone.

-I assure you of that, my friend!

-Every passing moment this gets more complicated, I'm not convinced

-Why did you have a Visa credit card, prepaid?

-I don't have cards, Mr. Martinez.

-The account statements of that card arrive at that address.

-That is not possible!

-Half an hour after the robbery, you deposited $3,000.00.

-That's not true.

-Now you realize why I'm interested in your private life?

-Do you mean to tell me that this woman is an accomplice to this conspiracy?

-You must realize that, if it's a conspiracy, those who want you to appear as the culprit will do everything carefully so that the investigations don't reach them. That damn woman must be involved in this.

-Don't talk like that about a woman.

-Don't you realize, the woman named Carmen, is part of this whole problem.

-I understand, now I'm opening my eyes.

-Did you have sex?

-Mr. Martinez!

-Did you sleep with her, yes or no?

-You are talking like a gang member.

-Answer the damn question!

-Yes, we had sex several times!

-Did you notice anything that caught your attention in it?

-I don't understand.

-You saw something suspicious on it, like a mark, a tattoo, her missing a toe, something you can take as a reference.

-Her three eyes.

-Now you really left me worried.

-She had a tattoo on her back, it was a large eye perfectly elaborated; it was the same as her own eyes.

For a few seconds I thought about what the young man had said. He was trying to remember where he had seen a woman with a tattoo of an eye painted on her back. That was something unique and I had to remember.

-Did the cat get your tongue, Mr. Martinez?

Who stole my identity?

-Why do you say that?
-It's just that when you talk about that whore's tattoo, you were speechless.
-Have you ever been infected with gonorrhea?
-Why the hell do you ask me that?
-I just want to see if I know that woman
-Do you know that wretch?
-After having sex with that woman, did you discover something strange about your penis?
-I'm going to go crazy!
-It is important that you tell me the truth, do not keep small things that could be of vital importance in this case.
-I've never had such good sex as I did that night, when we first went to bed.
-Did she ask you to penetrate her through the anus?
-Jesus Christ!
-I think I know who that woman is.
-Three days after we had sex, my penis began to smell bad and pus was leaking from the orifice, it was something disgusting.
-Did you penetrate her anus, yes or no?
-Yes
-Shit!
-What's wrong with you?
-Wait a minute, be quiet for a moment, let me think.

How small the world is, now he was totally sure he knew who that woman was. Three years ago, I had been part of one of my private investigations. She was the main target when businessman Silvio Reynoso asked the law firm, he worked for to investigate his wife.
I noticed that young Hank was surprised, scared and confused, so I decided to change my attitude and end that interview.
-We will do one thing.
-What?
-I must do some research before I decide whether to take the job.

-I don't know what you have seen in this case, but you can be sure that I am innocent.
-Don't worry, time heals and discovers everything.
-Mr. Martinez, please take my case, I am a victim.

I said goodbye to the anguished young man with the promise of seeing him again; it had been an exhausting day, I kept analyzing in my mind every piece of evidence that the FBI had, against Dante Antonio, who, according to my deductions, was the victim of a terrible conspiracy.
For the moment, I only had fragments of possible clues that had been left by the real criminals.

I had to stop by Mr. Dante Hank's house, to update him on the process; I had decided to take the case because now I had strong doubts about the guilt of young Hank, and that encouraged me to start a counter-investigation of the case. I said goodbye to the young man, leaving him with a tormented mind, almost on the verge of madness.

The next day, I passed by the residence where the young woman named Carmen supposedly lived, but I discovered that the house was empty; there was not a trace of her there.

I immediately left in the direction of meeting Mr. Hank, so that he could sign the contract that would allow me to continue in the investigation of the bank robbery.
I knocked on the door of my future client's father's house and he opened it immediately, as he was waiting for my visit; There we started the conversation:
-Mr. Martinez, a few hours ago, my son informed me that yesterday, you spent almost the whole day in prison, paying him a visit.
-Yes, we were analyzing the evidence of the case.
-Will you take the Investigation?
-Yes.

-That takes a great weight off my shoulders, Mr. Martinez.

-I will take the investigation on one condition.

-As you say.

-If you do not accept my conditions, I resign immediately.

-What you say will be done.

-They cannot leak any information we obtain, sharing or analyzing the case with another person is a violation of the contract we will sign.

-I agree.

-I warn you not to take the law into your own hands.

-Now I must ask you some questions.

-Go ahead, what do you want to know?

-Who is Diego?

-What about my neighbor?

-Tell me about him.

-I only know that he lives in the house across the street for about four or five months.

-Do you have your neighbor's phone?"

-No.

He wanted it all in that sense, he believed that there could be some connection with the neighbor named Diego and the woman who found his son on Facebook.

-Do you suspect that man?"

-What man are you talking about?"

-My neighbor named Diego

-I have a hunch.

-I haven't seen him for a few days.

-Wait for me here, let me verify something."

I went out the front door to go and take a look at the neighbor's house. I knocked on the door insistently but got no answer; I went through the back and realized that it was uninhabited. The furniture in the living room looked old, as if second-hand; It was evident that no one had lived there for a while. I retraced my steps and re-entered Mr. Hank's house, who was waiting for me in great distress; On his face he had the signs of panic.

-What's going on, Mr. Martinez?
-I definitely want to take your case.
-Do you suspect anything about neighbor Diego?
-Yes, I suppose that someone prepared a conspiracy against your son, using his personal information.
-I don't understand anything you say.
-Did you know that your son was in a relationship with a young woman?
-Once you told me about a certain Carmen.
-Before I got here, I passed by the address where she supposedly lived, but there is no trace of her there.
-My God, what's going on?"
-I think I know that woman.
-No way!
-This world is a little surprise box, my friend.

The Inquiry was taking shape; I was beginning to put the puzzle together. Now he would have to begin the difficult task of discussing or changing a guilty verdict in which there was much front-line evidence left by the criminals who committed the bank robbery.

I immediately signed the contract with Mr. Dante Hank, I called the owner of the house where Diego lived, with the excuse of seeing if he would rent it, but he replied that it was occupied by a tenant who was traveling and who had paid him a year's rent in advance.

He was beginning to understand that this apparently simple case could become one of the most interesting he had ever had.

This matter became dangerous; now I had to put all my knowledge into practice because here the powerful mind of a criminal, capable of committing a perfect crime, was vented, leaving a chain of evidence that pointed directly to a harmless middle-class young man, the son of a man who was not satisfied with the FBI or with what the evidence obtained by the feds showed.

Although in most cases the people imprisoned say they are innocent, there are some who spend a large part of their lives locked up in a cell without being guilty, for the simple fact of not finding someone who believes them or does what needs to be done in cases like these.

It was necessary to discover who the two people who completed the circle of the conspiracy really were: Diego and Carmen. There was no sign of them, I had to go into the houses they once inhabited to see if I could get any clues that would lead me to them.

I decided to wait for the researcher's number one accomplice: the sunset. When it began to get dark, I passed by the front of my client's residence, looking to detect any movement out of place around the house where Diego lived.

At that moment I detected something out of the ordinary; a powerful surveillance camera covered the entire front of Mr. Hank's house, focusing directly on the front of the suspect Diego's residence. I called my client on the phone from a corner near his house.

"Mr. Hank, I saw you put a camera in front of your house.
-You never know, you have to put security, look at what is happening with my son, I don't want to be caught off guard again.
-I think I was very clear with you.
-What do you mean?
-I do the investigation of this case, that's why you hired me.

-I'm not doing anything that interrupts your work.

-The objective of his camera is to watch Diego's house; please don't want you to lie to me, if we start with lies, I won't be able to continue investigating.

-Understand, Mr. Martinez, it is my son who is in prison, accused of robbing a bank.

-I understand, I will allow your surveillance on one condition.

-Which one?

-If you see any movement on that property, before you do anything, you should call me so that I can decide what is best."

-Deal.

-Now I will be clear enough with you; If he makes any move related to my investigation without consulting me, I withdraw from the case unceremoniously.

I wanted to make my position clear to Mr. Dante Hank, since, in previous cases, I have seen desperate clients get into the scenes of the investigation, even interrupting the course of the investigation.

I waited for the right moment to enter the uninhabited residence that the missing Diego had occupied. It was 11:00 p.m. When I got out of my car, which I parked at a safe distance.

I was wearing a black suit and bulletproof vest in case a neighbor mistook me for a thief and occurred to shoot me with some kind of deadly weapon. I was wearing sneakers in case I had to run, ropes inside a backpack that some researchers use in which we carry equipment that at any given time can make our work easier.

I had to hide to get in, but I noticed that there was a light on in front of the house. The bulb was about 100 volts, illuminating the entire area. I passed in front of the house for a moment to reconnoiter the perimeter where I would attack "doing this is advisable in this type of work" after my inspection, I proceeded with the attack.

I pulled out a small pellet gun, pointed the light, and only one click was heard. The clatter of the glass did not give me away because they fell on the grass; only the sound of the pellet impact was heard when it broke the glass of the bulb. I left that area for about thirty minutes and placed myself in a place from where I could see any movement that was made within my target. Everything looked calm, now he would move on.

I reached the front door and hid behind a leafy plant in the neglected front garden; The lock was large and thick supports; I would have to look for another part of the house where it was easier to enter. At that moment I noticed that the mailbox was full of advertising brochures; This was another sign that the inhabitants of the house were absent.

I turned around to go into the back of the property; The back door to the kitchen was made of sliding glass.

I took a scanner out of my backpack and turned it on to see if the house was protected with an alarm system, because if so, I had to turn off the panel of the safe or else, I would not be able to enter. The scanner immediately detected a remotely operated camera and alarm system, this was another clear indicator that I was in front of a person who was watching his every move, therefore, I also had to be very careful.

I programmed the device to deactivate the alarm, after opening the door that would allow me to enter the house that I would raid in search of information that would lead me to identify the man named Diego.

I had to decide whether to run away or stay inside the house when he forced the back entry; I put a hood on my head completely covering my face. Only my eyes were exposed, my outfit made me look like a black tube; Now I was ready, I would start forcing the door with a special hammer made for those purposes.

I inserted the tool through the edge against the wall; I broke the lock on the glass door, which quickly gave way. I immediately began a race of seconds; I passed through the center of the room at lightning speed and in the blink of an eye, I was in front of the alarm panel that sounded with the whistle of the first two minutes.

The equipment I placed began to copy the numbers on the screen, which I immediately typed to silence the detector device, which, by turning off its lights, allowed my nerves to calm down; At that moment, the video was deactivated by the scanner's grid.

I was inside the house in darkness; even so, I inspected the entire area. As I walked through the great room, I noticed that there was only some furniture that I had already seen in my previous inspection when I approached the house the first day, I visited Mr. Dante Hank.

My small flashlight shone every inch of the room, looking for evidence that would lead me to the suspect.

The house was almost empty, besides the furniture in the living room; in the kitchen only a refrigerator where I found a carton of milk with an expiration date of a month ago; another reason to think that Mr. Diego had left that house about 30 days ago. In the two rooms there was only one mattress without the necessary irons to make the bed; It was noticeable that this was a transitory place.

Although I didn't find anything that could help me identify the suspect, I was ready to leave, but suddenly, a soft noise caught my attention. I discovered that someone was trying to open the front door, but like me, it was impossible for him to achieve his goal; I felt as he headed towards the backyard, he was surely looking for an easier entrance. My stomach was burning and even though it was a cold winter night, sweat was running down my body. I would never recommend my research students to go into private property, but if you sit around waiting for it to rain, you will never see the rain fall as the popular story says.

The subject pushed open the door that I had forced; he opened it without any problems, as he had left it ajar in case she had to run away at any moment. I put on my mask again and hid behind one of the columns that divided the kitchen room, the intruder kept advancing with a terrifying firearm in his right hand.

I was in a very delicate situation, I could not hesitate, I had to decide no matter how risky it was; I had to come out of that difficult moment unscathed. The silhouette continued to advance inside the darkened house, when I had it close, I extended my arm and placed my small pistol on its forehead.

- If you make the wrong decision, you'll end up being eaten by worms!

Time stopped, the sweat continued to run down my body sliding down the middle of my two legs, for a moment I thought I had urinated from fright.

The individual was paralyzed; My soul returned to the body when the shadow said:

-Now I am in serious trouble with you, Mr. Martinez.

-What the fuck are you doing here, Mr. Hank?"

-It's a long story.

-It's better that we talk outside of here.

I snatched the revolver he was carrying and put it in my backpack; I pushed him toward the exit door in the kitchen, which was still open.

The night was dark, only a few stars could be seen illuminating the sky with their spectacular splendor, but that light was not enough to identify anyone. My client had committed a recklessness that violated the terms of our contract; He was aware of that and assumed what the next step was, so he apologized for having committed such an irresponsible act.

We cross the street and enter his house; There we settled our differences.

-I just want you to answer me one question, what the hell were you trying to do?

-The only thing I can say is that I deeply regret the stupidity I committed.

-It's better for both of you that I withdraw from your research

-I will not allow that

-You have no control over my actions, sir!

-I know I could interrupt or ruin your investigation, but if it is of any use, I beg your compassion.

-It will be of no use to me to threaten you again; This time we'll do something that will make you think twice before taking a step to meddle in my work.

-I don't understand

-I will let this one go, everything will be forgotten, but from now on, every time you get in my way during this investigation, I will charge you $25,000.00 as a fine, if you pay it, we will go ahead if you accept this condition, we will continue.

-Deal.

-No, we will do something better.

-What?

I took out the folder I had inside my backpack, placed it on the table and told my client to write in the contract, in his own handwriting, a note clearly specifying that, if he got back into my work or disobeyed an order, I would resign from being his investigator or he would pay the sum previously agreed. Without hesitation, Mr. Hank placed the note at the bottom of the second page of the contract, where he also stamped his signature.

In the long time that I have been working as an undercover person within organized crime, I have noticed that what hurts a person the most is having to correct a mistake with money, especially if the sum to be paid is considerable. I did this with my client because I was interested in continuing with this work that was becoming more and more interesting and dangerous and that at the same time, could become one of my best investigations

The night became long, I left in the direction of my house totally exhausted, my body urgently asked for a good rest and to release a little of the stress I had because of the unpleasant moment that my new client had made me go through.

"The perfect crime is not the one that is not solved, but the one that is solved with a false culprit".

Sir John Hurt- Arthur Seldom

Movie Quote: The Oxford Murders

4

CARMEN

It was 5:00 in the morning when my phone started ringing; I couldn't answer because I was taking a bath, but at the insistence, I went out half soapy to take the device; it was obvious that the caller did not want to leave a message, they wanted to talk to me at that moment.

-Hello!

-Attorney Julián Trenton of Orlando Florida is talking to you, I would like to have a meeting with you

-How did you get my phone?

-A colleague from Miami recommended your services.

-If it's not indiscretion, can you tell me, who is that friend who recommends me?

-It's better to leave it like that for the moment," he told me to keep it a secret, ha, ha, ha.

-There are no problems.

-When can you come to my office?

-As you know, my headquarters is in Miami, and to go to your office in Orlando, you would have to have a full day.

-I have a small office in Miami, where we can meet tomorrow

-Perfect, that's a good idea

-I'll call you after noon."

-I'll wait for your call."

I wrote this meeting down in my agenda for the next day, for after lunch.

No matter how busy we are, we cannot neglect our food, if we do, we will be forced to take breaks in the ward of a hospital.

The next day, as he said, I received a call from the lawyer to coordinate my visit to his office. After his beautiful secretary arrived, he invited me to go to his boss' office, who immediately extended his hand to greet me when I entered the office room. The man began by saying:

-I have a serious problem which, according to our mutual friend, you can help me solve.

With this approach, the lawyer began his conversation; It was obvious that he needed my services.

-Go ahead, I need the details to do an initial evaluation of your case to determine if we can really help you

-Two years ago, I married a lovely young woman named Carmen Loaiza.

-How old is your wife?

-When I met her, she was twenty years old, we married three months later.

-What do you think I can do for you?

-A few days ago, I started to have discomfort in my penis, it was an itching in the tube where urine comes out to discharge the bladder

"Did you go to the doctor?"

-Yes, and after doing some tests, he gave me a diagnosis that left me alarmed. I contracted gonorrhea.

After doing some explaining and talking about facts about gonorrhea, its causes and effects, I continued with my questioning.

-Your situation is difficult if you are married.

-How did I get infected with this disease?

-You probably had sex with an infected woman without using protection.

-Negative, I am a faithful man, I have a woman who in addition to being beautiful is ardent and young; I don't need to go outside for pleasure.

-Do you mean to tell me that you have never thrown a straw in the air?

-I only have sex with my wife.

-The million-dollar question would be, what would I be good for, in that situation?

-The one who infected me was my wife, she must be sleeping with one of the sons of bitches, of my friends.

-The fact that he has that disease, does not mean that it was his wife who infected him.

-Everything indicates that it was her and I want you to follow her for a month; If we find out that she is cheating on me, I will divorce her.

The man looked confused, upset, and disoriented.

-I'm not convinced that your wife is cheating on you, but if you want us to open an investigation, sign this contract and pay 50% of this amount upfront.

The lawyer saw the total sum he had to pay and without thinking twice, he took out his checkbook to make the payment. I asked him for a photo of his wife; he gave me information about the outings that his lady usually made from Monday to Friday; Saturdays and Sundays were spent with her husband who rarely left the house.

Carmen Loaiza was a very beautiful woman; she had expressive eyes that reflected flashes of light, with long eyelashes and very bushy eyebrows; tall and long-legged, round face and full seductive lips that would attract the attention of any mortal.

The woman started her day by going for a walk with her dog very early in the morning. She stayed at home on Mondays and Thursdays to do her housework, on Tuesdays, Wednesdays and Thursdays, she helped her husband with his clients' files. We began surveillance on the first Monday after we had signed the research contract.

Carmen's activity was ordinary, everything seemed normal. Seven days a week she left her house early to walk with Lebrón, her black Doberman; they always walked to a park near their residence.

It is said that, in Germany, Mr. Karl Friedrich Louis Doberman, 1834-1894, found a stray dog of unknown breed and noticed that it had interesting characteristics; he crossed it with the Pinscher, and this is how the Doberman breed was created

The Dobermans were named in honor of whoever created their race. They are domestic dogs, although they are often used as guardians because they are very loyal to their owners and jealously guard their belongings. It is said that Mr. Doberman confiscated goods and made compulsory collections, so he needed a large and ferocious dog to take care of him.

In the photos that I took during my research of Carmen and her dog while they were walking through the park, you could see the care and affection that she gave to Lebron, her dog, that was the only thing that caught my attention in this whole matter. My client's wife did not go out with strangers or her husband's friends; she was only seen accompanied by her dog.

The days passed and I felt worried, because I had signed an investigation contract with my client and so far, I had nothing to report to him; His wife gave no clue that associated her with a lover.

Carmen was distinguished using blouses with pronounced necklines both in front and back, which allowed you to see the striking tattoo of an almost perfect eye that she had painted between her back and neck. I had taken several close-up photos with my powerful cameras in which you could see the resemblance of the eye in the tattoo to the eyes on her face; It seemed as if she had a third eye on her back.

I called my client to make an appointment where we would review the results of my research; I was sure that his wife was not being unfaithful to him as he thought.

-Mr. Trenton, we have already been investigating your case for 30 days and we have not been able to find any evidence that leads us to doubt your wife.

-That motherfucker is cheating on me, you have to keep going, I'm sure she has a lover!"

Although he had a vague suspicion, he did not want to create problems between this couple who seemed to lead a harmonious life.

My client insisted that his wife was a whore, and since the client is always right, he could not doubt her words; I had to get on with my work.

-I want to exhaust a possibility.

-Speak clearly and directly.

-If you allow it, I can put several cameras inside your house

-He's crazy!

-The devices that we will place in all the rooms of your house will be connected to the Internet. You would have a secret password and I will have another that you will know, so that, when you leave the house, you put my password and so I can see what is happening inside your house; On his return he puts his password to cut the image leaving me blind and returning to his privacy.

I didn't know that was possible.

-Yes, it is a system that you can turn on and off at any time.

-Could you see every corner of my house from anywhere in the world?

-That's right.

-Are you supposing that the wretch who sleeps with my wife comes into the house when I go out?"

-No, it's something more complicated.

-You are a mysterious man.

-I just want to exhaust all resources to leave you alone.

-When do you want to place the devices?

-Tomorrow when your wife leaves the house, I want her to be near; I will take a technician who will only take 35 minutes to place the cameras and for sure, no one will notice their existence.

I had an idea going around in my head, but it wasn't very likely that my suspicions were true; Anyway, since in my research work, I had seen so many strange things, anything could be possible.

My technician placed the small cameras, some the size of a coin, attached to the ceiling and the color of it, it was impossible to see or detect. The device took the Wi-Fi signal sent to the satellite that deposited it in an Internet account that my office managed remotely.

When we talk about Wi-Fi, we refer to one of the most widely used wireless communication technologies using waves today where technology is dominating our lives.

A jealous man or woman sees ghosts where there are none, but sometimes life brings us surprises that we could only believe by living them.

On Monday nothing happened that could give us a clue that a lover was entering the house, but I continued with my strange suspicion. Finally, next Thursday at 8:30 in the morning the woman arrived sweaty from her walk, to which as usual, she was accompanied by her dog, the cameras recorded a totally clear image. She looked upset and suffocated; She began to take off her clothes from the moment she entered through the front door, she placed the secret code that was put on the alarm, and this caused me great concern. If it was in the morning, because it activated the alarm that was only activated when they were getting ready to sleep?

She took one of the sneakers she had taken off and threw it at the dog, who showed her his teeth in an attack plan. Nerves took hold of me as I saw the woman get on all fours, preparing to face the animal. She continued to take off her clothes until she was completely naked in front of the animal, which continued to show its enormous fangs when it opened its jaw to attack its owner who continued to challenge it.

My assistant and I approached the residence, we did the surveillance a few blocks away from the house and we saw on the computer screen of the car that we used for such purposes everything that was happening inside that house.

The female changed position with her back to the animal that climbed up from the back and took out its red penis to initiate a sexual act with its owner, in which it would penetrate her anus as if they were both animals of the same species

We could notice that the dog was trained to initiate sexual activity when she provoked him and undressed. The animal understood its owner's signal perfectly. The dog-woman sexual act lasted about twenty minutes, she roared with excitement and made noises she had never heard, the dog growled with doggy pleasure; It was hard to believe that this was happening before our eyes.

I had heard that some women performed oral sex on their pets and that they got used to the teachings of their owners, but I never imagined that I would see with my own eyes a sexual act of this type. He suspected that Carmen had another man inside her house, who could well be a friend, whom her husband mentioned on some occasion, but I never imagined that she had sex with her dog.

I took the video and immediately deleted it from the Internet database; I called the client to inform him that the investigation was over. He wanted to see me immediately so that I could show him the evidence. My assistant Alex and I showed up at the attorney's office where we met behind closed doors.

-I don't want you to be scared by what you will see next, these are things of life.

-Show what you have, I'm sure it's my neighbor who's sleeping with that bitch.

-He's wrong, his lover's name is Lebron.

-Shit, what a damn coincidence!

-What did he say?

The lawyer intervened to say:

-His name is the same as my dog, the damned man.

-It is with your dog that the Lord is unfaithful!

I said these words to say something while I turned on the computer that minutes later began to present the image with the sounds that still resonate in my ears.

-But it's with the dog!

I took the disk where I had the recording from the computer, handed it to him and left that office totally mute; My assistant was walking close to my arm because she was afraid that our client was something like his beautiful wife and would attack us.

The investigation had gone better than I thought, we were looking for a man and we found a dog that was the lover of his owner. A week passed and we didn't hear from the lawyer, but something worried me. It was to be expected that the case of a jealous man who intended to beat someone would have a different outcome; I made up my mind to do a few hours of vigilance to satisfy my curiosity.

We were near the house since 5:00 in the morning waiting for Carmen to take her dog for a walk as she did every day, but we never saw her go out. At that moment I had a feeling; I picked up the phone and called the Humane Society of the State of Florida.

-Hello.

-I want information about a particular dog.

-Tell me the name of the animal.

-I don't have it complete, but I think they call him Lebrón.

"What race?"

-It's a Doberman.

-Is it a puppy?

-No, it is a large, adult, black dog.

-Do you have the names of the owners?

-Yes.

"Tell me the name."

- Carmen Loaiza.

-One moment, please.

If something had happened with the animal, this was the institution that could give me instant information since they had a very complete computerized filing system. When the young woman who was attending me returned to the phone she told me:

-That animal was incinerated two days ago

-How?

-He died of poisoning.

"Who killed him?"

"It seems that he ate something when the owner took him for a walk.

"Doesn't that seem strange?"

-What do you know about this case?

-You're absolutely right, this dog was poisoned.

Who stole my identity?

I closed the communication and went to the office of attorney Julián Trenton. I wanted to ask myself some questions. He did not want to receive me, I don't know if it was due to embarrassment or lack of time, but he sent me a note with his secretary that said the following:

-If I need it, I know where to look for it, I am getting divorced and I assure you that in a month I will be a free man.

"That man intrigues me, Watson; He knows how to hide his emotions very well".

Sherlock Holmes

5

THE MOST WANTED

The main objective in this work was to identify Mr. Dante Hank's neighbor, the man named Diego.

I had controlled the camera system that my client had installed in front of the suspect's house, my assistant monitored all the movements that were made in front of the guarded house on the Internet, technology replaced human surveillance, a well-placed camera could do a better job than two investigators stationed in front of the target.

Nothing new was happening and that was why I took the second step risking a little trying to provoke some new situation. I requested a special search from a retired policeman, an expert in fingerprints who did some off-record work for me. He wanted to get fingerprints inside Carmen's apartment, and at the home of the man named Diego, without telling him that those properties had been abandoned by their tenants.

El Tuerto, as we called the fingerprint specialist, had lost one of his eyes in the line of duty, when he worked in the police. A criminal fired his pistol, seriously wounding him and making this brave policeman lose that important organ, which is why we gave him the nickname of the One-Eyed. When we met, I immediately said to him:

-I want you to do me some work tonight.

-What is the secret?

-I don't want curious people to see you entering those properties.

-Are you sure I won't have problems with the authorities?"

-I swear.

I managed to get my friend, El Tuerto, to show up at about 10:00 p.m. at Carmen's apartment.

I had the scene ready, I opened the door as if I lived there, to give confidence to my friend who, making use of his specialty, would begin one of the most meticulous works I have ever seen. We had to get the fingerprints of the mysterious unknown young woman, named Carmen.

After three hours searching for footprints, we became worried, because the only ones found were that of young Hank.

-Are you sure someone else lived here?"

-The story is long to tell; so, says Mr. Hank, "his father."

-Someone is lying, I assure you of this.

-Supposedly, the owner of the apartment was the woman, my client's son was only the boyfriend, who came to visit her to sleep with her and then return home.

-I have a lot of experience in this work, and I advise you to open your eyes. If another human being lived here who was not your client's son, that person is an expert in erasing traces and the intention was only one.

-That only the footprints of Dante Antonio Hank, the son, appeared.

-It's possible.

"Tomorrow we'll do another similar inspection in the other direction, there's nothing more to do here, friend.

-What other direction?

-I have another job for you.

This matter was becoming more and more complicated, without a doubt the people behind this conspiracy, if there were any, were true professionals of organized crime or belonged to high-caliber intelligence services. He was almost certain that behind these robberies there were other powers; This did not look like an investigation into a simple bank robbery.

The people who are directing the strings of power sometimes commit acts against citizens regardless of the damage they cause, to achieve their objectives.

I had no time to lose, the next day I informed my client that I would do a new search inside the missing suspect's house. This time I decided to warn him to prevent him from appearing again wielding a gun and complicating things.

My friend. "The One-Eyed One" concentrated on his work, applied powder everywhere and used powerful binoculars that detected any footprint from a distance "if there was one inside that house". After two hours of work, the former policeman said:

-I caught you red handed!"

-Did you get anything?

-I have a clear fingerprint with which I will identify who lived or entered this house.

-Let us pray to all the saints that they are not the footprints of our neighbor.

-What?

I was just thinking out loud.

The last person who had used the bathroom was reckless enough to raise or lower the toilet lid, according to what my friend said, this was a perfect footprint.

-This wretch, if he is a man, must be homosexual, an intelligence agent or was imprisoned in a federal prison.

-What leads you to think that?

-I also have my secrets.

-Please, don't tell me now that you're gay.

-Work finished, I won't say a word, you will have your report.

I was nervous when I observed the One-Eyed man put the fingerprint found in his system to verify this type of evidence electronically, everything was going very well until the ex-policeman wiped the sweat from his forehead to tell me:

-This wretched man's name is Diego Sandoval. I will write down the data and other matters in this notebook, with this my work is finished.

Now the pursuer could be the persecuted, he had to hide very well because he was out in the open.

Diego Sandoval: He began his criminal life at the age of 20, when with a gun in hand he entered a bank asking everyone to throw themselves on the ground because it was a robbery. An FBI agent, dressed in civilian clothes who was in line to cash a check, took out his regulation weapon which he was carrying concealed and shot the robber, who, with a gun, scared the group of customers who threw themselves to the ground to avoid being riddled with bullets in the shootout that took place when the federal agent's bullets began to come out.

The assailant received a wound in the chest, this knocked him down immediately, the agent of the

FBI pounced on him and said:

-If you want to die unhappy, make a move!

A few minutes later, the bank was filled with police officers; The paramedics took the assailant to the hospital who a few moments ago had a group of people terrified. The congratulations exhausted the patience of the young agent Manuel Fernández, who was aware that he had done a good job.

For this crime, the assailant Diego Sandoval, after recovering from his war wound "as he said", was sentenced to 15 years in prison and was assigned to a prison in California, since his last known address was in that state. The Judge made that decision, because no close relative of the assailant had been found.

After getting the voluminous report from the public system, which contained the background of the disappeared, the next step was to leave for California, with the assistance of an acquaintance, to try to see the files of the prison where this man who was now being pursued by my private investigators served his sentence.

"How deep a mystery is the mystery of human freedom. If it were given to us men to know the why and how of this mystery, we would already know the why and how of all things".

Anonymous

6

A PROFESSIONAL SACRIFICE

California, a name of European origin, is the fifth oldest state in the United States.

The name California is said to be derived from the name of the regent of a fictional paradise dominated by black Amazons, Queen Califia.

California has a population of 38. Million inhabitants and occupies an area of 410,000 km2, with these figures we can say that California is one of the most populous states in the United States and the third largest in size, after Alaska and Texas.

I took a flight to California, in search of completing the information that would lead me to obtain data to follow the trail of this dangerous criminal, bank robber, who for the moment was missing. I had to start my search in the house, "prison" where this person lived who was imprisoned for several years.

A well-known politician who owed me some favors put me in touch with the director of the prison where Diego Sandoval was imprisoned. Prisons are dark places, where people of care live. Both prisoners and guards carry frustrations that spread like a virus within the complex prison population.

I introduced myself to the guard at the front door; I informed him what my needs were and who I would visit on this occasion.

-I have an appointment with Mr. Anthony Frade, the director of this prison.

-One moment, please.

The man took my ID and placed it in front of him, while he typed the data on it with a computer keyboard. When he had finished, he rose again from his seat and said:

-Stand in front of that window, I'll take a picture of you.

I let myself be guided without putting up resistance; my only purpose was to talk to the man who had the files, the history of every day that my suspect "Diego" had spent in that prison. I could tell that everything was arranged when they made me go into a small room where a man came to pick me up and only said: Follow me

We arrived in front of a metal door; The guard who accompanied me said:

-Visit entering.

The door opened and we took a corridor that led us to the center of the building where the phrase was repeated:

-Door opening, visit entering.

After walking a long way, "I think to impress myself with the security that was in the place," the last door opened that led to the office of the man who ran that place.

Unannounced, a man in a gray suit, white shirt, and red tie appeared in the center of that room, as if he had broken through the wall. I never imagined that in that office there could be a simulated door that led to a bathroom, which was for the exclusive use of the director; the bathroom was a kind of hiding place.

The subject extended his huge right hand to shake mine; I immediately rose from my seat to respond to his greeting.

My friend, the one who connected me with this man, warned me to be very careful with him, because he had some very heavy games with people who were interested in his work. He looked at me with the eyes of inspection to say:

-Sit down, please.

-Thank you.

The director turned and closed the only door that was the road to freedom. When I heard the frightful noise of the door closing, I felt a fear that penetrated to my bones; a fear so intense that I cannot describe. I tried to control myself, I knew that my confinement was momentary; I was just there paying a visit.

The mere fact of being subject to the will of people who only knew how to give orders and make them be carried out, altered my nervous system. These guards acted as automatons; Those men had to be guided by a manual of conduct which they had to follow to the letter, which forced them to comply with what the director ordered. After taking some documents that he had on his desk he told me:

-Nice to meet you, Mr. Martinez.

-The pleasure is mine, Mr. Frade.

-Our mutual friend informs me that you are interested in the confidential files of the criminal Diego Sandoval.

-Yes.

-Did you talk to Diego's lawyer?

-No.

-First mistake, Mr. Martinez

-Do you have the name of that lawyer?"

- His name is Julián Trenton.

For a moment I was breathless, I thought that destiny had something in store for me again, that is why I always say that nothing is casual, that everything has a reason in our lives. He only had to connect the dots, he wanted to verify that in the case he was investigating in favor of the young Hank, his girlfriend, the woman with the eye tattoo on her back, was the ex-wife of Diego Sandoval's lawyer. I would not say any of this to the director of the prison since I came in search of information and not to give what I already had in my file. Trying to disguise it, I took out a notebook and wrote on it the name of the lawyer of the ex-prisoner I was interested in finding.

-Do you have anything else to tell me?

-No, sir, just ask your permission to see those files.

-What do you want to know, Mr. Martinez?

-I look for a needle in a haystack.

-Let me give you a little information so that you wake up and do not let yourself be surprised by the damn rat called Diego Sandoval.

-Our mutual friend warned me that you are a very busy man with many responsibilities, it is one of the reasons why I do not want to take too much time from you.

-Are you determined to find out who the unfortunate Diego Sandoval really is?

-Yes.

-Today is Thursday, the weekend will be good to play golf with our friend the congressman, who commissioned me to be his collaborator.

-Today is a wonderful day.

-You will stay in my jail until Monday since I have some obligations this weekend and I will have to leave the city.

This man looked like a madman and when he spoke, the emphasis in his words and his cold gaze tormented me.

Worst of all, I was now in a tremendous predicament; If this sadistic degenerate thought that I would spend three wonderful days in prison in his jail, for the simple fact of wanting to go through some dirty papers, he was crazy.

-I can't stay in your jail for that long, sir.

-In this place only, my voice is heard and what I say is done; Now you are one more of those who, when you enter here, become my guests.

-I'm sorry to contradict you, sir, but you can't force me to stay in your building for that long.

-We'll see who's right, Mr. Martinez, you came from the warm beaches of Miami to look for a congressman from this city to help you meet with the director of this prison.

-Up to that point everything is fine, but no one has broken the law.

-Our friend, the congressman told you that I always give more than what is asked of me.

-He spoke wonders about you, he said that you were very cooperative when asked for a favor and he also said that you were a tremendous son of a bitch.

-Mr. Martinez, I will be a collaborator with you, I will help you with what you want to know, I am sure you will thank me. See you soon.

The man disappeared through the same door he entered; it closed leaving the wall without any traces that there was a door there. Seconds later, I heard the sound of a door behind me; It was the door through which minutes before I had entered, a guard appeared and guided me to the one I knocked: secret hiding place, the room did not have much space, for two people it felt cramped, without windows, walls painted dark green. Things weren't going the way I thought they would, but I had no choice but to follow in the footsteps of the prison guard who told me:

-Put on these clothes, I'm going to take you to cell number "11"

-You're wrong, you'd better get me out of your damn prison before that son of a bitch closes the building!

-We can do this in two ways: You act as a prisoner, or I will lock you up here for three months on the charge of facilitating the escape of one of the prisoners.

-This is an outrage!

-I'm just an employee who follows orders, if he doesn't do what I'm telling him I'll get him into a problem that he never wanted to be in his life!

For now, I was in the lion's den, and I had to wait for things to take a different turn. I put on the kimono that was used as clothing in the prison, then followed the prison guard again.

There were cages with prisoners on both sides of the corridor, inside rooms protected with huge bars that indicated to visitors that they would be under arrest. This was not a dream, when the guard took a large key to open cell number "11" I realized that he was really a prisoner. This time the subject said out loud:

-Visit entering cell number "11"!

The din of laughter left me confused and nervous. Ha, ha, ha, the laughter of the prisoners sounded in the cells that made up the pavilion; This infernal sound was like a whip that mistreated my body.

That looked like a horror movie, the mockery came out of each of the cells on the first floor of the building that housed about 1,700 prisoners of selective profile, which translated into common language meant that I was in a place where in any carelessness, they could murder me from behind or rape me while I slept,

What I was most worried about at the time, in the worst case, was if someone identified me as a private detective and divulged this information to the prison population, I would surely be beaten up and paralyzed or wheelchair bound for the rest of my life.

In my new room there was a two-story cabin, with a thin mattress, a white sheet, the bible and a toilet. Fate is unpredictable, a few hours ago I was in a luxurious room at the Marriott Hotel, luck had changed me, now I was in a place pending everything, because any carelessness could cost me my life.

Time passed without me noticing, it was like having a nightmare while awake. I heard a noise in one of the corners at the top of the cabin and then the shadow of someone's head appeared that looked like a skeleton from the Roman catacombs. Then listen to his powerful voice; It was difficult to connect that sound with that figure.

-I suppose you are my new companion.

I was cold as an ice floe, there was another prisoner in the cell where I was being held, I answered correctly.

-Not for long.

-I understand.

-What does it comprise?

-They left you here while the plane carrying the prisoners passes through this area and picks you up.

-You are right.

I had a roommate, the man who was lying on top of the cabin was thin, with a big head and a macho voice, I thought an alien had appeared on me.

We started a conversation that went on for a long time, we looked like two old friends who were meeting again after many years.

It was the best thing to do, I had to get used to my new situation or start crying non-stop until I saw what my luck would be.

-My name is Brando the Italian.

-I am Ángel Martínez.

"With you, that makes three companions I have had in this prison

-That's good.

-What?

-Odd numbers are good luck.

-Do you mean to tell me that you have brought me good luck?

-Maybe.

-My old colleague was taken yesterday by order of the director to send him to the third floor.

-Follow the number three behind your destiny, Mr. Brando.

-The first companion I had for more than seven years was the biggest son of a bitch who has passed through this cell.

-Why do you say that?

-The unfortunate Diego Sandoval, he is a lucky man.

Hearing that, I stopped breathing for a moment and felt my heart freeze, but I had to keep my new friend from realizing that his comment had impacted me in that way.

The mad director of the prison had played a joke on me in bad taste, imprisoning me next to the man who was a cellmate of the man he was persecuting and for whom I risked coming to this place in search of information.

-I believe in destiny.

-If you have time, we can talk.

-Mr. Brando, we have nowhere to go, the best thing we can do is talk about what we like.

-I like your point of view.

Things were following the way he wanted to go, without having to insist, my companion began to talk about the deception of his former cellmate.

-I was sentenced to 25 years in prison for a robbery I carried out in New York, against a Banco Popular... When I arrived at this prison to serve my sentence, I found a young man who had just served fifteen years in prison for having committed a robbery at another bank in Miami,

Florida.

-The pressure system makes unforgivable mistakes.

-Why do you say such a thing?"

-I don't understand how it occurs to them to put together in the same cell, two prisoners who committed the same crime.

-In that you are right, because that is why we became friends.

-Are you still friends with that man named Diego Sandoval?

-The only thing I received from him after he left here was a photo that looked like a postcard where he appeared hugging his daughter, in a restaurant owned by her.

-Was your friend Diego transferred by the director?

-That's why I'm telling you that this wretch is a lucky man.

-I don't understand.

Due to problems of occupancy in California prisons, the Supreme Court of Justice of the United States decided to release thousands of inmates. A similar order had been issued in 2009, but at that time the State of California appealed the Court's ruling, alluding that the released prisoners constituted a danger to the population.

In August 2009, three federal judges ordered the release of 4.000.000 prisoners in two years.

Late last year, California appealed to the Supreme Court to overturn the sentence.

Yes, I remember that decision: The Supreme Court of the United States ordered the State of California to release thousands of prisoners to alleviate a serious problem of overcrowding. In order not to violate the constitutional rights of prisoners, due to non-compliance with new constructions and transfers out of the State or other means, many of them had to be released before serving their sentence. The ruling was approved by five votes to four.

The economic situation of California had generated for some years a situation of spaces to house inmates in its prisons. There are currently 148,000 inmates housed in 33 prisons designed for about 80,000 people.

-Was that what caused your friend Diego to get out of prison?

What precipitated the matter was when two prisoners were stabbed in a riot of more than 150 inmates in a maximum-security prison in the city of Sacramento, California. Guards had to use pepper spray and fire several shots to regain control, prison officials said.

-If I get out of this, I won't forget you, my friend.

-But that's not all!

-Is there still more?

Human Rights Watch presented a report that says that maximum security prisons in the United States, which house a minimum of 20,000 inmates, are a source of suffering, humiliation and physical, mental and emotional destruction.

According to one report, inmates spend 23 hours a day locked up and held incommunicado in cramped, windowless cells, where food is smuggled in through a hole.

They have no right to phone calls or visits and when they leave the cubicles to shower or walk for an hour a day, they are stripped naked, searched, handcuffed and led away by guards armed with electric batons.

-Everything was in favor of your old companion, Diego

-The scandals are innumerable on this subject

-The Department of Justice is investigating Virginia's maximum-security prisons, after learning of two cases of inmates who died in strange circumstances, one of them committed suicide six months after being released, another, who was diabetic, died when he suffered seizures, and the guards denied him his medicines and beat him with their electric batons. In Illinois, four inmates at the Tamms Maximum Security Prison have filed a class-action lawsuit in court alleging they are victims of cruel and disproportionate punishment.

The desperation of one of them, "Azor Rasho", reached such a level that in August 1998 he tried to commit suicide by cutting his wrists; the guards reacted with total indifference that, in their presence, "Rasho" began to eat the torn flesh of his own arms. He was taken to the infirmary, where he was treated, but, when he was returned to his solitary confinement cell, he lifted the stitches and drank his own blood.

-This is dreadful.

-Did you know, Mr. Martinez, that the American Civil Liberties Union (ACLU) has sued the Youngstown Penitentiary, where three prisoners have just committed suicide and psychotherapy sessions are administered with the inmates chained to a pole, for violation of civil rights.

What happens in U.S. prisons is inhumane

I wanted to continue motivating the prisoner Brando the Italian, as he was called in prison, to continue talking, but fatigue overcame me. It was 10:00 at night. I had spent a terrifying day, which caused me to fall asleep in the lower part of the cabin that I shared with my new friend in that maximum security prison.

I was half asleep when I heard a loud sound, I woke up scared without being clear where I was, after a few seconds I remembered that I was imprisoned with a dangerous criminal in a maximum-security prison in California, United States. My cellmate was dressing in a hurry, I could barely take my feet out of the improvised bed.

When he realized I was awake, he said, "Devil."

-You slept like a little bird. Still half sleepwalking, I answered:

-I was extremely tired, I spent part of the night dreaming of a man like the devil.

-What did you dream about?

-I asked the chief of hell how he could rob a bank.

-I can answer that without being the devil.

-That's something I've always wanted to know.

-I can tell you what the steps are to take to commit the perfect bank robbery.

-I would like to hear it, go ahead.

-The first thing you must do is select three accomplices who are criminals that you can trust, because you have to avoid being snitched on or keeping the part of the stolen money that corresponds to you. I don't like the idea of having partners in these matters because if things go well, you must share everything with them, however, if the work goes wrong, you have the advantage of being able to reduce your sentence by betraying one of the three who would like to plead not guilty.

-The second step is to make a list of banks that are in remote areas of the city to choose the loneliest of all.

-In step three, you take care of getting clown costumes made up with a lot of paint.

-Step number four is very interesting; You must leave some clue that incriminates someone, so you will take the pressure off while you escape.

-The fifth step is of vital importance, you must buy several rolls of adhesive tape, preferably gray and of good thickness.

-You must keep in mind that the number six is bad luck, you must get toy guns, so, if you are caught now and have the toy found, the charge or sentence will be less. This is not 100% certain because if the prosecution is good, they will get prison for 35 years, which is nothing, compared to what happens if the jurors are white or old women who play on Sundays with their grandchildren and think about the interest that their retirement accounts earn.

-Never forget step number seven; underneath all that clown costume you should have normal clothes on: white shirt, jeans, shiny shoes, preferably black "inside clown shoes" and glasses that should be in your pockets for when you leave the bank; you put them on as soon as you take off your costume; That way you will completely and immediately change your appearance.

-Now comes step number eight. You enter the bank fully disguised and entering step number nine, you order with a very loud tone of voice:

-Everybody on the floor, this is a damn robbery, and if any wretch wants to die, let him try to move!

-In step number ten you confirm what you said earlier, but with more force and looking at who could be your first hostage or victim who is already lying on the floor. He asks a question in front of his face.

-Do you want to die, son of your damn mother?

-If possible, give him a little kick in the middle of the belly, so you will have the atmosphere dominated.

-Now comes the good part, in step number eleven, you have to say a word or phrase in English with the correct pronunciation. Like: "Yes, or What is your problem, man?" With this you will confuse the investigators, they will look for people who speak English perfectly, giving you that, greater chances of not being discovered because at the time of chasing the thief, they will go in search of an American.

- Mr. Brando, do you mean to tell me that with those eleven steps I perform a perfect bank robbery?

-No, you have to take step number twelve, preparing to continue gaining ground, you must also say some words in German or another language, with these techniques you will drive the FBI detectives crazy, who will look for Europeans or people of other nationalities.

-In step number thirteen, after everyone is already terrified and petrified on the floor, including the unarmed security guard, you proceed to take a sum of money out of the safe and place it in the bathroom, then you put the hostages in. You give the indication that they do not talk to each other and much less that they look at each other and to make sure of that, put one of your accomplices to take care of them, if you are lucky for this one then the police will have already arrived, but don't worry, it is part of the plan.

-Step number fourteen is to wait for the police to ask you to release the hostages and to turn yourself in claiming that you have no escape and so much more.

-You just pick up the phone, talk to the police headquarters and tell them that you are the guy who is robbing the bank and that you want to make a deal with them; Tell them that you will release the hostages if they comply with each of your requests to the letter.

-Step number fifteen is the most fucked up of all, here you ask the police for a small black refrigerator with chrome views, six pairs of Nike sneakers, sixty-nine family-size pizzas, processed meats and extra garlic to feed all the hostages "believe me, you're going to need this, the extra garlic is indispensable"; You also ask for twenty liters of soda, a brass of red paint and a small brush.

-In step sixteen and six, the police will be uncomfortable with you because of your multiple requests. If they don't want to give you the refrigerator or the pairs of sneakers you requested, don't worry, those are not so important, but if they refuse to give you the pizzas, the red paint and the brush, then it is true that you get upset; you curse the mother of the one who speaks to you and tell her that you will kill all your hostages because of her; also tell them that you will let all the media know this and thus, the families of the hostages will blame them and want their heads; After that warning, it is 100% certain that they will supply your order.

-I didn't know that robbing a bank required so many things

-Wait, there are still a few things missing

-Shit, what a difficult job!

-Now I'll explain the next step. When the pizzas arrive, you feed the hostages and you eat too. Then you take the brush and paint the numbers 1, 2 and 3 in the middle of the chest of each one; Then you free three of the painted hostages who have eaten pizza and spread them with garlic. After an hour you tell him that if they bring you a mouse in a shoebox with holes in it so that it can breathe, you will free three more hostages.

Here's the catch.

-The three robbers who have already filled the boxes they have inside the bank, with the money that was in the safe deposit boxes, will prepare to leave. The thieves would never talk about the theft because they are criminals who are not interested in revealing their affairs since they could be very harmed.

-Now you will have to go slower; If you took an hour before to answer when you took out the three painted hostages, this time you have to take half an hour more because since the other hostages are locked inside the bathroom, no one will find out what is really happening; The police will get desperate and ask you to release the other 3 hostages as promised. Surprise! There you go out with two companions, with scared and confused faces. The good thing about this is that you will have garlic breath and painted with red paint just like the first three hostages you freed.

-In the last step, when you leave, the police will question you, but you won't know a damn thing about what's going on inside the bank so they will never think that you are responsible for all that.

- This is great, just great!

-Wait, the auction is missing, after the questions, you just get lost in the crowd and that's it, now you will be the proud owner of a large amount of money and beautiful clothes.

-After three or four hours pass, the SWAT team will enter, breaking everything and screaming like crazy; The real thieves will be out and happy because, in short, their plan was a success, and they would not be accused of anything.

-But that plan could bring you back to where you are now.

-It is possible, but I am perfecting it.

Brando the Italian stopped talking for a few seconds waiting for me to continue inquiring about his plan to make a perfect bank robbery.

I didn't believe in the perfection of the plan; I thought that committing a criminal act like that anyway was a crime that could bring him back to jail where he was now. Seeing that I didn't continue asking, he stood in front of me and said:

-Let's go to the public toilets.

-Why do you wear all those clothes?

-Here you must protect yourself, if you show too much, you can be attacked and raped.

-I will follow your advice!

In this institution the danger was always latent, the Mexicans dominated almost the entire prison, the Central American gangs occupied the other territory of the property. I was very lucky, Mr. Brando the Italian, he was highly respected for being the oldest prisoner in that prison and because he was a close friend of the Italian mafia boss in New York.

-We'll go out down the corridor when the doors open, if someone looks at you don't take your eyes off them, keep it while you can, I don't want them to think you're a weakling, because if you did, you'd be an experiment rat for those wretches.

I was taking a huge risk, I felt like a rat inside a maximum-security prison where I was looking for information about a suspect I was chasing.

That is the work that a private detective must do who seeks that the results of his investigations exceed the expectations of his clients.

We were walking down the main hallway to the restrooms when a man with tattoos all over his body stared at me. I could not look for trouble within that enclosure; I kept walking, pretending that I wasn't paying attention to anything, to divert attention away from that man.

I followed the instructions of my roommate, I did not leave his side at any time, we entered the dining room and there I lost sight of the man with the tattoos who was the person who had noticed my presence the most in that prison.

I noticed a movement on the right side of where I was sitting; The prisoner sitting next to me stood up and went out like a frightened chicken to the opposite side of the table.   My cellmate stopped eating and looked up to warn me of the approaching danger. I was confused and scared, a cold sweat came out of my pores and ran all over my body; I had a feeling that, in this hell-like place, the worst was about to happen. The man with the tattoos sat down next to me and said:

-They say you're the new one.

-That's right

Answer without looking at him, forgetting the first commandment of the prison law which is: "Look into the eyes of your opponent" because if you don't, you would be demonstrating superiority or fear

-I want you to be my wife!

-When?

-Immediately let's finish eating.

Without thinking twice, I lowered my hand and grabbed what made a small lump in the middle of his legs, luckily what I grabbed was one of her testicles which I twisted strongly so that he would feel the inexplicable pain that we men feel when this part of our body receives a blow or is mistreated in some other way.

He wanted to get up from his seat, but I didn't let him, and I gave him a tug that took his breath away. He was paralyzed, sweating profusely; He kept jerking harder every time he tried to move.

At the table that was intended for eight people there were only two men seated, side by side, like two lovers on a beautiful spring day. The comments made in low voices by the others about that fact could be heard; It was my great opportunity to ridicule my opponent in front of others.

-Open your mouth! I told him

-I swear I will kill you wretched!

I gave him such a hard tug that he opened his mouth at once and put a piece of bread in it; The subject was surprised at my audacity. At that moment my salvation appeared, a group of guards appeared in front of our table and the leader of the group asked:

-What is happening here?

-Nothing, sir.

I went ahead to answer by letting go of the testicle of the man with the tattoos that was red as a tomato about to rot. The law enforcement officer continued to insist

-Niki, are you okay?

-Yes, sir

I got up from the table patting my opponent Niki on the back, and said in a low voice:

-Next time I swear I'll rip it off you.

I left in a hurry before the devouring looks of everyone present, I had come out triumphant in my first meeting, but the difficult thing was to keep being the leader for the time I was locked up, especially because my opponent had many conditions to win if we faced each other in a fight.

I noticed that all the inmates who passed me by and greeted me with bowing their heads; A rumor had spread that I was a European assassin who had various levels of martial arts training and that, on one occasion, I took out a policeman's heart with my own hands and could not be blamed for the fact for lack of evidence.

It was Friday afternoon, I knew that I could not keep that image for long, so I insisted with my cellmate to get the information I needed about Mr. Diego Sandoval, from him in a short time.

-You're right about what you said about that Diego

-What are you talking about?

-Leaving here was a real salvation for that man.

-I think he is now robbing banks with his two friends.

-Which friends?

-We were a small group of four assailants who devised how to carry out the robberies.

-Did the other two also manage to get out during the problem that arose because the prisons were full?

-Jerry Corona and his half-brother Sanfor Carpí, left a few days after Diego, surely, they must be together fabricating their operations to commit other perfect crimes.

-Is it very difficult to organize a perfect crime?

-That Diego, he made some perfect scenes; I bet on your job when it comes to robbing a bank.

Now he had to find the postcard that Diego had sent him, with the photo taken in her daughter's restaurant; it was the only thing I needed to complete my research.

When we entered the cell on Friday night, I took the Bible because I thought it was the most appropriate place to keep something like that. I opened it and began to leaf through it slowly.

In Luke 15 I found what I was looking for. the postcard with the photo of the damn "Diego and his beautiful daughter" smiling with a glass of wine and probably toasting to the happiness of being together. Without wasting time, I inserted the postcard into my pants, but I was struck by the title of the gospel that spoke about the lost sheep, when it explained in the sacred Book the following:

-A large number of people came to Jesus to listen to his words, the Pharisees and the Pharisees.

-Master of the law they murmured, criticized.

-This man receives sinners and eats with them, Jesus realizing the situation and said to them:

-If one of you loses one sheep out of the 100 you have, doesn't he leave the other 99 in the field to go in search of the lost one until you find it? And when he finds her very happy, he puts her on his shoulders and when he arrives at his house, he gathers friends and neighbors and tells them:

-Rejoice with me, for I found the sheep that was lost to me! I declare to you that in like manner there will be more joy in heaven over a single sinner who changes his heart and his life than over 99 righteous people who have no need of conversion."

This passage of the Bible comforted my spirit, we went out to the aisle for dinner looking in all directions to see where I would receive the next of my lovers. The man with the tattoo and his associates were close to the wall where we were walking towards the dining room. He was marked, I could not see him very well because it was not possible to face five individuals armed with two knives and strong arms that would crush my fragile body in less than a rooster crows "as my grandfather used to say".

He could not show fear, it was the only way out of that encounter with the devil in his lair; I continued walking to meet face to face with my attacker who stopped, looked everywhere and said:

-I want to announce to you that at dawn you die!

-That is yet to be proved, my friend.

I answered him to continue walking as if nothing was happening there, the man wanted to jump on me, but one of his companions prevented him from doing so because he knew that if he attacked me in the middle of the corridor it would go very badly for us; The guards of that prison saw and heard everything that happened there. I still wonder how I got out of that hell alive.

It was 10:00 p.m. on Friday night when the lights went out, my roommate remained silent, he did not want to give his opinion so as not to be involved in the tremendous mess he was in. He pretended not to understand, he ignored me because he knew that very soon, I would be a corpse; I knew the kind of enemy I had gained.

Accompanied by darkness, a group of ten security agents entered the main corridor of the prison, walking with strong steps without caring what the prisoners who were in the double occupancy cells on both sides of the corridor thought or said. When they arrived in front of the door of cell number 11, one of the guards took out a large key while they shone a flashlight into the room; The guard who led the group, in a very low tone of voice said to me:

-Mr. Martinez, gather your belongings.

I jumped out of bed, almost fell into the arms of that man dressed as a guard; On his face was a clownish smile. It was the director of the prison who entered my room, once there he asked:

-Do I have to do anything additional inside this cell?

-It is not necessary, sir, everything is in order here.

I answered without hesitation so that Mr. Anthony Frade, the warden of the prison, would realize that I had gotten what I was looking for.

-Let's go, it's getting late.

We came out of that hell, and I did not say goodbye to Mr. Brando the Italian.

We arrived at the office of the head of prisons who treated me very courteously. He apologized to me for the tasteless joke he had made on me by putting me in jail for two days making me face a dangerous criminal who swore to murder me that night.

After freeing myself, I stopped by the hotel where I prepared to leave for Miami, Florida, where I now had to dedicate myself to the hunt for the man who, in addition to knowing his background, had a photo that would help me in the search. This time he had to organize a different strategy because it was necessary to make the FBI aware of what he had discovered about the man named Diego

"It is a capital mistake to theorize before possessing data. Insensibly one begins to distort the facts to make them fit into the theories, instead of fitting the theories into the facts."

Sherlock Holmes

7

THE FEDS

After arriving in Miami, I began preparations to visit the FBI facility in South Florida

When you request a meeting with the feds, you have to be prepared to give them as much information as possible about the case to be dealt with and if you think that they will give you a single clue for your benefit, you are very wrong.

The agents are trained to put you as deep as possible inside four walls adorned with strong bars where they will take all the information you have, it is their way of proceeding, "everything for the agency".

It is not my intention that my readers misinterpret my opinions about the FBI, so I clarify: This institution has very serious agents who do their job fully but be clear that a police officer will always be a law enforcement officer, he is in that position and was trained to enforce the law.

I can testify that my good relationship with this agency has borne important fruit due to the audacity, intelligence and capacity of a man who for many years stole the admiration of the criminal leadership of Florida, for complying with all the agreements he made with them to get them to go over to the side of the Law. This FBI super-agent is called Manuel Fernandez, "Fictitious name of: M.F."

I arrived at the FBI facility and in the cubicle at the entrance on the second floor, I asked the receptionist to announce me to Special Agent Manuel Fernandez, who after receiving me, ushered me into a room where we would have a private conversation. Going into detail immediately:

-I am doing an investigation in a case in which I believe, you have an innocent person who seems guilty of robbing a bank.

-What is the name of that person?

-His name is Dante Antonio Hank.

-I know that young man.

-He is an excellent young man.

-What do you have to tell me about this case? I reviewed the evidence; without a doubt he is guilty of the fact.

-I think he is innocent.

-Prove it to me, but in this case, you don't want to be too clever.

-I have only one suspicion.

-With that I cannot get to court to prove the innocence of this man and you know it.

-I think it is your duty to review a case when there is an injustice.

-Don't come at me with nonsense, you know I'm very busy, don't waste my time!

-I notice you are irritated.

-That's right.

-I think you need a little sex.

-Something you can't give me!

No matter how close you are to an FBI agent, they take care of their position, because the efficiency of their work depends on it.

-We will do only one thing in this meeting.

-Go ahead.

-I'll leave you some names and if you're interested you can call me.

-What are you talking about?

-Do you remember a man named Diego Sandoval?

I hit him where he wanted, when he heard that name, his face gave him away, he couldn't help but look surprised. He leaned on the back of the chair where he was sitting; When he assessed the possibility that I might have information about this character, he asked me:

-What do you know about that man?

-Are you interested?

-We could say that the FBI is interested in knowing how much you know about this criminal.

-I'm on your trail.

-You're coming to the wrong place, my friend.

-This man is a dangerous bank robber who was imprisoned in California, along with three classmates of the same class. The curious thing about the case is that his companions: Jerry Corona "el negro" and Sanfor Capi, who are half-brothers, were released from prison a few days after him. Brando the Italian, a prisoner whom I visited for a few days in his cell, told me that they rehearsed to commit the perfect crime, robbing a bank when they got out of prison.

-Shit, I always underestimate you friend!

-Look for the updated files that you have on these three robbers and ask permission from your superiors so that we can discuss the case on equal terms.

Without saying anything else, I left the room where we were assembled; The agent knew that if he spoke so properly it was because he had more than a suspicion. If you want the FBI to take you seriously, just blurt out something about what they have in their files.

Now I had other things to do; when I went out to the streets I located the restaurant of Diego Sandoval's daughter, I took some photos of the parking lot and then studied what would be the best place to do surveillance and see the cars and people that arrived at the place.

After that fieldwork, as the agents call this type of work, I decided to leave the area to study the latest developments in the case.

If I put surveillance on the place and they detected me, my life would be in danger because these criminals are very special, they are willing to kill when they feel trapped or persecuted; On the other hand, he didn't want them to hide.

The best option would be to conquer one of the two employees who did the parking work. The cars of the visitors to the restaurant we were interested in were either too flashy or too luxurious. I had to study which of the two parking employees was the one; A good researcher must have everything well calculated before taking risks.

I started by doing an in-depth investigation of the two parking lot employees and I decided on one who was a student of Criminal Justice, at Nova University, who was of very limited economic resources and did that work to pay for part of his studies since he had a half scholarship granted to him by the University.

We had to approach the young man very carefully because we didn't know what familiarity or friendship he could have with the owners of the restaurant, so I thought that my assistant Alex, helped by a skirt above the knees, would have to show off more than just his beautiful legs.

The lady in her brand new Mercedes-Benz car, C63AMG Sport Sedan 2015, valued at $58,000.00 , rented, of course, waited in the middle of the block from where she could totally see the movements of the two employees in the parking lot; immediately the companion of his objective took care of it, my assistant Alex rushed out in search of the young man, who, seeing it, stood in front of the car door to open it; This was a golden opportunity for a good researcher.

Alex looked at him with a smile, then took his left leg out of his carriage with the sole purpose of making his lens look at his heels and the opening of his legs that showed colorful panties, from the brand "Victoria's Secret".

This skill of the researcher left him out of control, which she took advantage of to tell him:

-If possible, I'd like you to take care of my car yourself.

-Okay miss, I'll park it in the "VIP" area

-As you like.

The young woman got out of her brand-new car leaving the engine running, after finding herself near the door of the restaurant and staring at the young man who was still watching the well-shaped girl's toning, she asked him:

-What's your name?

-John.

-Thank you.

John followed with his eyes the walk that the young woman took towards the center of the establishment.

The lady was seated at one of the tables and ordered everything she found appetizing from the menu; She took an aperitif whose name she never knew because she preferred that the waiter who served her surprise her with an exquisite drink.

She left a good tip on the table and left the place; she signaled to John to come closer.

-How much does parking cost?

-$20.00 missed.

-Could you accompany me to my car?

-With pleasure.

The walk was not very long so my assistant Alex had to make the most of it. The young man played with the key fob of the supposed owner of the car; He approached the car and opened its door from a safe distance.

-John, do you believe in luck?

-I don't like to gamble.

"Would you believe me if I told you that today is your lucky day?"

-It's possible.

-When is your day off?

-Whenever you want, miss.

-Ha, ha, ha good sense of humor, I like that.

John, thought that he had just made a conquest, adjusted the hair that covered part of his face, with this he sent the lady the message, he understood that she was flirting with him, provoking and offering an approach for sexual purposes.

-I have Mondays and Tuesdays off

-Can we have a coffee together, next Monday?

-Of course!

-Can you give me your phone number?

Without answering, the young man took out a ticket of those he used to give the numbers of the cars he parked, wrote down his cell phone number there and passed it to the beautiful lady, who took it with a smile of triumph that left John totally captivated.

The contact was made, now it was just a matter of waiting. We had to put surveillance in front of the restaurant where it was very possible that Diego Sandoval and his criminal friends would appear.

For the investigation to bear fruit, it required resources which it could obtain from two sources: Mr. Dante Hank "or" the FBI. Pick up the phone making the first call:

-Mr. Hank, little resources are required, the investigation is having magnificent results.

-How much do you need?

-Not to bother him often, I think he would be fine with $25,000.00

-I want results, no matter what I must spend.

-Do not be confident, sir, I remind you that those who believe that money can do anything, are undoubtedly willing to do anything to get it.

The second source for funding could be the FBI, so I proceeded to call my contact, who would surely be very intrigued with my investigation into this criminal. I went into detail about how important it was to see each other:

-Can I see you?

-I have been waiting for this call for several days, which, without a doubt, is to request resources to pay for your adventures.

-I have in my hands something more than suspicions, if you collaborate with me, I can give you that group of criminals on a silver platter.

The FBI agent did not have to add much, or make too many calculations, he knew very well that a good investigation cannot be carried out if you do not have resources translated into money, cash.

-I don't want to deny that we're interested in the people you told me about, but I want things to be done our way, not yours.

-We both have the same purpose.

-Do you have anything in particular?

-Yes.

-You know I can't go to the bosses with only suspicion.

-At the moment I am working on the identification of the suspects.

-Do you have them located?

-I have them under surveillance.

-I get you resources on one condition.

-Which one?

-That when you see or locate Diego, let me know, it is very important for this office to have that criminal under surveillance

-Deal

-How much money are we talking about?

-$100,000.00 is needed for operational expenses

-You are crazy!

-I'm not.

-With all that money I would fill the prisons of the State; I would arrest criminals by trucks.

-I'll talk to another government agency, I see that you, the best, are dying of hunger."

The FBI instills in its employees that they are the elite of the federal government, so when you want to get something out of them, you have to tell them, very cautiously, that there are others who can do what they don't do and give them a little bit of professional jealousy so that they can give in.

-I'll talk to get you half of what you ask for.

The bureaucracy that the State Department has in Washington is the cause of the terrorists hitting us where it hurts the most.

-You know how the strings of power are handled; everyone wants to shine with their own light.

-When you have the resources, call me.

-Wait a minute!

-What did I do now?

-I'm not your bank, I want to be very clear about that, I'll get that money, but I want a very detailed report without forgetting to write down everything about the development of the investigation.

Now I had what it took to follow in the footsteps of my target, I had to outsmart and be more careful than all of them, agents and criminals.

I called my assistant Alex, to continue with the surveillance project that we had set up in front of Diego Sandoval's daughter's restaurant. The appointment was made, all that remained was to put the finishing touches on the planning of the match. We had to take care that John didn't become a double informant for us.

Alex and John confirmed a date, which the young man assumed was to start a romance. My assistant had the green light to act depending on what were the motivations and the interest that, in his opinion, this young man could have in the case when the conversation took the direction of our interest.

At the meeting, John and Alex treated each other with confidence and a lot of familiarity, as if they had known each other for several years.

-How do you feel John?

-Very well, miss.

-I don't want you to call me miss again, my name is Alex

-Thank you.

The young man, although confident, looked a little nervous, showing shyness when answering Alex's questions.

-When I met you, you told me that you didn't believe in destiny.

-We talked about that.

-Remember.

-Yes, I remember now.

-Sometimes we have opportunities that we miss for different reasons.

"That means that you will offer me some opportunity.

-I like to talk to intelligent people.

-Can I be honest?

-That is one of the qualities that I like in a man.

-When I met you, it changed my life, I fell in love with you at first sight, like a fifteen-year-old.

-That's not bad.

-Do you think so?

-Yes, love is the most beautiful feeling.

-Why don't we get straight to the point?

-What should we discuss?

-I don't understand, it was you who said you were interested in talking to me.

-That's not true.

-What did you want to tell me?

-I said I'd like to have coffee with you.

My assistant was testing the young man, waiting for the right moment to start with the topic we were interested in discussing. Coordinate the strategy of the surveillance that we would do in front of the restaurant.

-That's right, you only said that.

-How much do you earn in your job?

-Do you work in tax matters?

"No, ha, ha, ha, I'm just curious.

-Why?

-An intelligent, elegant, and educated young man like you should do another kind of work.

-Like which one?

-I work in the security department of a law firm, and I would like to have you in our group. I see a good future in your aura.

-What a surprise!

-Which one?

-I didn't know you were a witch.

-I only see the future in the people I am interested in.

-I am a part-time student and I have some knowledge about the things you do in your job.

-Now it sounds more interesting. What do you study?

I knew everything about the young man, but this question was very important to take the conversation in the direction I wanted, Alex.

-Criminal Justice at, Nova University

-If you're interested, I can ask my boss to give you a job that you can do in your spare time."

-I'm interested.

-This is the address of the office where I work. I'll wait for you there on Monday after 10:00 in the morning.

-I'll be on time.

-One more thing.

-Yes.

-I ask you for discretion, try not to comment on my offer.

-Count on my silence.

The bait was already on the hook, if the fish stung it we would have a spy in front of the restaurant in less time than I had thought.

The conversation of the young people continued in the direction desired by John, who continued to think that love had come to him without knowing how. He had in front of him a woman more beautiful than the one he had imagined in his fantasies, when he dreamed that she ran over that beautiful body from head to toe and felt the contact of her moist lips, which trembled with pleasure, when they brushed her legs imaginarily, that we could call luck.

On Monday morning, all attention was focused on the arrival of the future employee. Young John entered the lobby, the secretary asked him to take a seat and then announced

his arrival. After about 15 minutes of waiting, the young man went to Alex's office, who greeted his visitor with an effusive hug.

-Wait a minute, I'll call my boss.

Alex came out of the hallway to let me know that John had arrived;

immediately, in the company of Alex, I went to the office where he was. He got up from his seat when I appeared at the door; That showed that he was in front of an educated person.

-My name is Ángel Martínez, I am Alex's boss, she tells me that you are qualified to work in our institution.

-Yes, sir.

-The first thing I tell you is that the work we do is extremely confidential so you can't talk to anyone about what we do.

-You can count on my discretion, Mr. Martinez.

-What I just told you means that if we find out that you have told someone about your new job, you will be fired without hesitation.

-I understand, sir.

-You will report directly to Alex. Do you have any questions to ask me?

-No, sir.

We had the missing link to find the whereabouts of Diego Sandoval and his accomplices.

I instructed Alex to go slow in this matter so as not to let him know our intentions right away.

Who stole my identity?

"When an innocent person is punished, an evil man is born."

Victor Hugo

8

THE DAUGHTER OF THE MOST WANTED

Digna Sandoval had graduated from the prestigious University of Michigan with a medical degree. This is a public university in the United States, located in the state of Michigan, whose main campus is in Ann Arbor and has other minor campuses in Flint and Dearborn. It was founded in 1817, twenty years before Michigan officially became a state.

Despite being a public institution, the University of Michigan is known for the high fees paid by students; Scholarships for foreign students are the most expensive in the country.

The strange thing about the case was that this young woman, three years after her graduation as a doctor, had ventured into the field of gastronomy by setting up a luxury restaurant in Miami Beach. The establishment had a fixed clientele of people from high society, who frequented the place in search of good food and exquisite attention.

The beach area in Miami Beach is visited every year by about 25 million people from different parts of the world.

Miami's climate is subtropical, cool, with mild, humid summers and cold, dry winters.

Digna Sandoval was scared when her mother took her to prison to meet her father. The young woman strengthened her bonds of love with her father, in such a way that her mind and behavior were tied, there was not a day that she did not have some reason to think about her father, Diego.

Our investigation showed that Digna Sandoval bribed a California state politician with one million dollars to include her father on the list of prisoners who would be pardoned for lack of space in the state's prisons.

We collected all the possible information about this woman with bulging eyes, medium height and wide hips, who stood out in her walk with movements that any man could pay attention to.

Their bank statements showed high balances; these documents were furnished by John, our new undercover agent operating within his establishment. We confirmed with different sources that she was bisexual, had a girlfriend who was a bank manager and a policeman boyfriend; the latter complicated things because her boyfriend could put her in contact with the judicial system leaking information of utmost importance creating an incalculable bribery path since in Miami he has an impressive history of corrupt policemen so when a policeman appears at an investigation scene and it is in Miami you have to take the first alerts although that happens only in some cases.

This super woman was powerful because of the money she had, her political and police relationships and the vigilance she maintained to protect her father and the criminals he directed, but since we had her intervene without her realizing it, we had a little advantage over her jobs or immediate plans.

We had to carefully direct John, who because of the excitement of doing the job of a spy could spoil everything if he allowed himself to be discovered. The young man was very enthusiastic in his first two weeks in our office. We had him busy working on the analysis of a case we were pursuing against a tobacco company, about a study published on the

Internet by the American Journal of Public Health that reveals that tobacco companies have withheld information about the presence of deadly radioactive poison, polonium 210 PO-210 in tobacco and tobacco smoke.

With this cover or entertainment, sometimes Alex put some obligations on her that were the ones that really interested us. He called to take some action that was required in the case.

-Give John the information of the four people we are interested in: Diego, Sanfor, Carmen and Jerry

-Is it very risky to make it known about everything?

-Just show her the photos of the suspects and never tell her that the owner of the restaurant, Miss Digna, is Diego's daughter.

-Okay, boss.

The less information you give an informant, the more you get from them. Young John was very helpful to us because of the valuable information he brought us from the guarded place. He began by drawing some important correspondences such as: The reconciliations of the accounts of two banks, especially accounts with balances of $3.5 million in Bank of America and $1.7 million in Chase. When I obtained this information, I was very uneasy.

I made the decision to analyze the mode of operation that was used in the robbery where our client, Dante Antonio Hank, had allegedly acted. Alex, I didn't understand why we were spending time on something unimportant, but I didn't share his opinion.

-On the day of the bank robbery, in which young Hank was involved, two customers had asked to reserve the sums of $375,000.00 and $225,000.00, which they would pick up around 10:00 in the morning.

This situation was the reason why there was so much money in cash when the robbery was carried out. Now I must investigate if those two clients are the same ones who carried out the assault or if they were related to it.

"Boss, do you mean to tell me that when someone is going to cash a check or make a withdrawal for a large amount, they have to call the bank a day in advance so that they have the money available?"

That's right, the bank asks for that money from the Federal Reserve, who send it in an armored truck, before the customer "who for some special reason requested cash" arrives at the branch to withdraw that large sum.

-We have to discover the planning they are doing to make the next assault; it is where we have to work.

-I am almost sure that Digna is involved in her father's affairs.

-This makes me think, which banks would be your next targets?

-These two banks must be investigated.

-Why do you think they are the possible targets?

Those criminals are planning another robbery, and the logical thing would be to have an account in those banks or to have an employee of those institutions as an accomplice.

This case had us on our nerves, we saw conspiracy everywhere, and we thought that the crime would soon be carried out. I had to fix my attention on Friday because most bank robberies in the United States take place on Fridays between 9:00 and 11:00 in the morning. That's a conclusion that FBI experts reached, after analyzing robbery statistics for 2010.

In almost all cases, according to FBI data, robbers use the following scheme:

They arrive at a bank branch and demand that the ATMs hand over the money by threatening them with weapons. Thieves often state their requirements in writing, in notes that are passed on to employees.

In 2010, there were 5,546 bank robberies and other financial institutions in the United States, according to data the FBI released Tuesday, April 5, 2011. The highest number of robberies were committed in California, 805 robberies, while Texas ranks second with 464 bank robberies.

The amount of money stolen in 2010 exceeds $43 billion, of which only $8 billion has been recovered.

We had to pay attention to any detail that would lead us to detect the presence of the criminals we were looking for. I was struck by a robbery where the police announced on their radio frequencies that they were looking for the thieves who crashed their vehicles into the window of a Gucci store, located in the shopping center [The Village of Merrick Park], shortly before dawn on that Monday.

According to police investigators, after hitting the windows of the establishment, the criminals stole dozens of bags, whose prices fluctuate between hundreds and thousands of dollars.

Three vehicles were seen speeding away shortly after the 5:23 a.m. incident. The estimated value of the stolen items has not yet been determined by police in Coral Gables, in Miami-Dade County, the report said when I got it.

After police in nearby cities alerted them to what happened, Miami police reported that they found a vehicle full of Gucci merchandise in their area, said Sgt. Janette Frevola, spokeswoman for the Coral Gables police in Miami, Florida, United States.

One man was taken into custody and is being questioned by authorities, Agent Frevola said. Coral Gables detectives said they hoped videotapes from surveillance cameras at some of the mall's stores would help them in the case.

Anything was possible, but this was not the way a professional thief operated, we consider this to be done by beginners who were looking for a few bucks. Everything had to be investigated, that was one of the reasons why we listened every day to the frequency of the police in search of clues that would lead us to where these criminals had a presence.

"The funny thing is that being outside prison he was an honest man, straight as an arrow. I had to go to prison to become a criminal."

Tim Robbins

Movie Quote: "Life Sentence"

9

A NEW ASSAULT

We had surveillance on the two banks where Digna Sandoval had her accounts; we watched from 9:00 in the morning until 4:00 in the afternoon; There was a researcher at each point. Everything looked normal because of the reports that came into my office.   What did surprise us was when John told us that he had identified the man named Diego, who, to his surprise, was the father of Digna Sandoval, the owner of the restaurant where he worked.

Immediately Alex received the call from his employee, we left for the place where the criminals were gathered; They were in one of the back rooms of the restaurant. I approached, totally disguised with a great wig with strands of hair painted white pretending to be an old man full of gray hair, totally harmless, pretending to be a beggar or homeless man who lived on the streets.

John, he gave me the key to the car in which Diego and his companion arrived, who turned out to be the lover of the Doberman dog. Yes, it was Carmen Loaiza, the ex-wife of lawyer Julián Trenton.

In the parking lot I found a Porsche 911. Carrera 4 GTS, 911 GTS family, 3.8 L boxer engine. With power of 408. HP at 7300 RPM, the one I checked everywhere.

Whoever drove this car was a professional, since he only had in the glove compartment the document of the place where it was rented.

The meeting on the night of September 17th lasted about four hours. There was a banquet of food and lots of laughter, in a totally private atmosphere. Only two women entered the room: Digna Sandoval and Carmen Loaiza, who served the three guests.

We did not know the reason for the celebration, but what I was sure of was that very soon these criminals would act. I placed myself in a strategic place to take some photos of the guests at the feast. When it was 11:00 p.m. they all left at the same time, which was a big mistake by the leader of this group because a photo where they all appeared together, linked them to each other if, in the future, one of them was arrested.

My infrared camera, with night view, was in charge of doing its job, taking photos in the dark. They left in two cars, Alex followed one while I followed the one, we were most interested in, the one driven by Diego Sandoval; the sexy Carmen accompanied him. They took a totally desolate road, they were heading towards the Florida Keys, this they did with the aim of detecting any intruder that was attached to their tail. When I realized their purpose, I decided to let them go. I could not let these thugs discover me, letting them go was part of our strategy according to the experience accumulated in other surveillance or surveillance.

On the morning of Friday, September 24, when I woke up, I thought that I had not heard anything about the criminals under investigation, but at 9:00 in the morning my phone rang insistently; apparently my assistant Alex had a serious problem.

-What's going on?

-We have these wretches cornered!

-Speak clearly, I don't understand.

-Turn on the TV and you'll find out.

Like a hungry lion, I jumped to grab the TV remote and find out what was happening.

There was an assault in progress right under the nose of one of my investigators, who was talking so fast I thought he had a nervous breakdown. The news read as follows:

"Hostage taking reported at the Bank of the United States"

Cable News Network. CNN Miami. The robbery of a bank in Coral Gables, Florida, has turned into a hostage situation and police are cordoning off the area near the University of Miami, local television reported today. Authorities surrounded the bank after a man entered claiming he had a bomb; Police said this is a hostage situation. According to the report of the television channel 7 WSVN, according to the police, the man entered the Bank of America branch at 8:15 a.m. on Friday, September 24 and refused to leave or talk to the authorities.

Police closed the vital US1 Avenue in both directions.

Students at the nearby University of Miami were instructed to stay away from campus.

The criminals arrived at the scene at about 5:00 in the afternoon; They had the plan to kidnap a person inside his house, the surveillance was constant, because they had to wait for the right moment guided by what was drawn on the map. It was 7:00 p.m. when the guard reported that a woman was leaving the apartment of the man he was guarding and who was sure that she was Gladys, the mother of the main target, an employee of the bank that they had selected to rob.

All surveillance is boring and dangerous; Whoever watches risks being seen by anyone who sticks their head out of a window. If the careful observer thinks that it is suspicious to see a man or woman sitting for a long time inside a vehicle, it may occur to him or her to call the police, with this possible action his or her surveillance is over.

Time passed, it was 11:15 PM, and the father of a bank employee, whose name was Juan Uscamayta, was in the living room of his apartment which he shared with his wife and son.

He was in the living room, in front of the television, watching the latest news, when someone knocked on the door. Without any precaution he went to the door which he opened confidently because he thought it was his wife who was returning early from her work, where she did night shifts at a nearby hospital.

The guns placed in front of his face terrified him. The intruders knew exactly what they were looking for.

-Where is your son?

-I don't have children.

-I'll repeat the question one last time, if you don't answer truthfully, it will be the last thing you hear in your life, you old shit! Where is your son Juan, the one who works at Bank of America?

A thick, black pistol remained in front of the old man's face. It was too late to hide his son who was in the room getting ready for sleep. The young man, when he heard a man talking to his father in a threatening way, jumped out of bed and took the phone, but he did not have time to call the police because a colored bandit had already put a gun to his head.

-If you don't want to die, put the phone down!

Young Juan was pushed out of his room and taken to the living room where his father was, sitting on the sofa with eyes bulging with fright. He thought that those three individuals who entered his apartment had intentions of hurting him or robbing him.

It was midnight on Friday, September 24, when these events were unfolding in an apartment neighborhood in the Nob Hill complex, 9800 Southwest 88th Street, in Kendall, Florida.

The assailants moved as if they knew the area well and were very confident; This worried the terrified victims who did not know the motive for that run over until the leader of the intruders said:

-This is an assault, I don't want to hurt you, but if you don't cooperate, I swear it will be the last thing your eyes will see." I'll kill you; do you understand?

The old man, a man who had more experience than his son, preferred to keep quiet so that the subject would not continue with his threats, but the son, completely nervous, said:

-You can take everything, but please don't hurt my father!

He had made the first mistake. When you are in a dangerous situation in front of any criminal, never let him know what your weakness is because that will be the one that the attackers will use to pressure you.

The group of Assailants realized that the father of the bank employee was the point where they would have to squeeze to get good results. The leader of the group said:

-We want the money from the bank, nothing will happen to your father, but you have to calm down." We have a long hour of work left and this young man will have to do the easiest part of all this.

The strong, masked man who led the group of criminals spoke slowly and gave very clear instructions; He confirmed his intentions and said that under no circumstances would he give in. Jorge Uscamayta, Juan's father, was tied hand and foot with ropes; The same procedure was applied to her son, and they threw them on the sofa in the living room where they were all gathered.

Hours passed while the attackers prepared food that they took from packages that one of them brought on an outing he made. After the first five hours of martyrdom had passed, inside the assaulted apartment, the attackers began to move.

From a cardboard box, they took out a black vest that contained some wires, two batteries that gave current to a circuit of small Christmas light bulbs that turned on when they pressed a remote control, which increased the panic in the two men tied on the sofa.

The device was placed like a shirt on the body of young Juan, in the presence of his father, who almost died of a heart attack because his blood pressure did not stop rising.

At 7:45 in the morning of that fateful day the leader of the criminals said:

-We'll go in the direction of the bank at 1540 South Dixie Highway in Coral Gables, the two of us will go with you, if something goes wrong, I'll order your father to be killed and the bomb we've planted will destroy your body and that of everyone near you.

-You don't have to be so cruel to us, don't you realize that my father is nervous, and this can cause his death?

-He'll die anyway if it gets out of hand.

-What do you want from me?

-We will leave you at the door of your bank, you will go directly to the manager, you will lift your shirt and give her these bags and when she has it full of money, you will go out to the door, give it to my partner and close the door of the bank again

-I think I can do what you ask me to do. What assurance do I have that you will not press the button on this bomb?

-The only thing I can offer you is my word, if you don't believe me, that's your problem.

There was no way out, you had to take the risk, the bank teller adjusted his bomb vest and dressed in a white shirt, black pants and red tie, just as he wore every day to go to work. With two of the three assailants, he left the apartment leaving his defenseless father tied up under the surveillance of a black man who would kill him if Diego Sandoval, who was running the operation from hiding, ordered it.

The wall clock showed exactly 8:00 a.m. when the two assailants got out of the car in the parking lot of the bank building along with the terrified young branch employee.

The road became long, sad and disturbing; An endless number of terrifying ideas passed through the young man's mind as they made their way to the building where he worked.

His heart began to pound, he was not so worried about what he was going to do but about what might happen to his father, if things didn't go well.

Again, the man who directed the operation gave precise instructions:

-I'm calm, I know you won't do anything that will endanger your father's life, and in case you forget, yours isn't worth half a cent if you don't follow my orders to the letter.

-If you keep your word, I'll do my job.

The young man replied in a trembling voice

-You have three minutes from the moment you enter the Bank, to talk to the manager, fill the bags and get to the door.

-He's crazy, that's a very short time!

"Here things will be done as I say!"

-I will try to do it in that time

-When you show the bomb to the fucking manager, remind her that if she calls the police, she will never get out of her damn bank alive.

-She won't call, I promise.

-Remind that bitch, I'll be listening to her on the closed circuit of the bomb you're wearing, if by chance she hesitates for a moment, I'll blow them all up, leaving their bodies in little pieces scattered all over the building.

-Things will be alright, calm down man

-I hope so, for the good of everyone.

The car door opened and young Juan got out of it, who had a bomb tied to his body under his shirt. The criminal, from the front seat of young Juan's car, waited to see the results of the operation.

The young man was filled with courage when he knocked on the door of the bank, waiting for one of his colleagues or the same manager who arrived at the doors every day to open it for him from the inside.

7:00 in the morning. Nerves dominated him; At that moment, one of the cashiers who saw her colleague knocking to enter, went to open the door for him.

Juan just said hello and continued as a direct robot to his boss's office, who was organizing some documents to fax to the headquarters in California.

Bank of America serves customers in more than 150 countries:

Argentina, Australia, Bahamas, Belgium, Brazil, Canada, Colombia, Chile, China, France, Germany, Greece, India, Indonesia, Ireland, Italy, Japan, Malaysia, Mexico, Panama, Peru, Philippines, Singapore, Spain, Switzerland, Taiwan, Thailand, United Arab Emirates, United Kingdom, United States, Uruguay and Venezuela.

The current Bank of America is the result of the merger between Bank of America and Fleet Boston Financial. With this merger, approved by the authorities in the U.S. in April 2004, the second largest bank in the United States and the second largest bank in the world were formed. Prior to this merger, Bank of America, then headquartered in California, and Nations Bank, "headquartered in North Carolina," merged, forming the first truly national bank in the United States, with offices from coast to coast and with a presence in dozens of countries around the world.

The banks that, through their previous mergers, make up the current Bank of America, have been institutions with personnel who over a period of more than 220 years have put their energies into forming their foundations. These Banks were established at different times and in different places, yet they have all shared a common purpose: to help their communities succeed and achieve their dreams. In order not to bore the reader with banking statistics, we will continue with the story.

Once inside the building, Juan, the bank employee, stood in front of the manager; she raised her head to say:

-Good morning, Juan.

-We have three minutes to fill these bags with money, if we don't or if we call the police my father will be killed and we will blow up when this bomb explodes.

-My god!

-Robbers have a remote control in the parking lot, if we don't obey they will blow up the bank with all of us inside.

Without wasting a second, the woman ran down the corridor that led to the vault where they had the money stored, she took out the key which fell to the floor because her hands were trembling with fear. The young man calmed his boss by saying:

-Please calm down, if we give you the money everything will be fine.

The woman looked at him for a few seconds without saying a word, took the key again, put it in the lock of the door of the gigantic safe and opened it quickly since they only had the bars on; The door secured by combinations had been opened at 7:30 in the morning to withdraw the money that the ATMs would use during the day.

They quickly filled the bag with wads of dollars in denominations of 100, 50 and 20 just as the assailants had requested.

Immediately Juan took the bag and ran to the door to deliver the order, which was caught by the black man named Sanfor Carpí, who with giant steps, without showing that he was in a hurry, entered the red Ford

Mustang car, owned by the young Juan Uscamayta.

They drove away from the area leaving at a normal speed complying with all traffic rules. Everything was going as the geniuses had calculated. Inside the bank, a chilling scream was heard that electrified all the employees who were in the assaulted premises.

-Throw yourselves on the ground, he's got a sneaker!

To support what the manager said, Juan took off his shirt and showed them the device they had made him wear. They were all so nervous that they forgot to set off the alarms. The security guard who was in the bathroom and had just come out, when he saw the robot man standing in front of him, his intestines betrayed him and he was given an order that he could not control. From what was seen coming out of the hems of his pants it had to be fecal matter, it was obvious that the fright caused him instant diarrhea that, to top it off, it stank up the atmosphere. His feet stuck to the ground and he just took out his revolver and said to the frightened young man:

-Don't move!

The employee carrying the bomb only said to the man who pointed the revolver at him almost to the point of firing:

-Stop shitting your pants and call the police, asshole!

The man walked around with the gun in his hand not knowing what to do; He got behind the first column he found to protect himself from the attack that, in his opinion, a bank employee was carrying out. Finally, the manager activated the first alarm she found on her way looking for a way to protect herself, then she took the phone from the office next to the safety deposit box, got under the desk and dialed 911.

-Come quickly, please!

The operator who saw the address of where they were calling from on her screen realized that there was an assault in progress; He flipped the switch to send the signal to all the police patrol cars that were near the scene. Juan looked calm, he was convinced that, if he gave him the money, the thieves would not detonate the device; What did worry him was his father, who, even if he were released, would be dying of fright thinking about what could happen to his son.

Immediately patrol cars and personnel from the bomb squad of the city of Miami began to arrive, along with members, dressed in civilian clothes, carrying weapons on their waists and gold badges that identified them as FBI agents, the situation was clarified because the experts were in control.

On the morning news, headlines appeared that left everyone in front of their televisions uneasy:

"Incredible robbery at Miami bank"

A robbery is taking place right now, the assailant or assailants are holding an undetermined number of people hostage.

There is no information yet on whether a "Negotiator" has begun to dialogue with the criminals to get them to drop their attitudes.

A team of masked bomb disposal specialists is at the scene. According to footage from the WSVN Fox 7 television channel, which has a helicopter in the area, there are a large number of police officers outside a Bank of America office, located in Coral Gables, across from the University of Miami Campus.

The UM study center alerted the students, by sending text messages, of the situation that is being experienced in the vicinity of the University Campus, so that they leave the place peacefully for fear of shootings with the assailants, who are inside the bank.

Members of the Miami police anti-explosives unit, as well as negotiators specialized in hostage situations, are at the scene.

We believed that the assailants were inside the institution and that would satisfactorily end our investigation because surely one of the three assailants we were investigating would deal with the authorities seeking a reduction in sentence if they found him guilty of the robbery.

When the second press release came out, all our hope fell to the floor, we saw on the news what was really happening inside the bank branch.

"Fake bomb, to rob the Bank"

The kidnappers managed to flee with more than $1,100,000.00, at the end of the day, the robbery aroused multiple suspicions when it was determined that the bomb used was fake.

On Friday at about 10:00 p.m., Juan Uscamayta, 26, a teller at the Bank of America branch in Coral Gables, was still being questioned by investigators. Coral Gables Police Department Chief Richard Naue said the suspects apparently tampered with a remote-controlled detonator and sent Uscamayta inside the bank.

"They told him they had a detonation device"

-Get as much money as possible and bring it.

The establishment had not yet opened its doors to the public, but the manager, whose identity was not revealed, was already inside.

"It is not unusual to use an explosive attached to a vest to rob a bank," said agent Dena Choucair, spokeswoman for the Federal Bureau of Investigation "FBI". There were bomb-making materials in the device, I can't divulge what materials they were.

The government agent indicated that the alleged explosive had been placed on Uscamayta's back, leaving some wires and metal in front of the young man's body to make it look like it was a real bomb.

After a call at 8:10 a.m., to the 911 emergency line, agents of the Coral Gables Police, the Miami bomb squad, the FBI and the Bureau of Alcohol, Tobacco and Firearms "ATF", surrounded the bank and cordoned off several blocks, which unleashed traffic chaos in the vicinity and Southeast 57th Avenue, near the University of Miami campus.

Faced with the danger of an explosion, the bomb team sent a robot, while negotiators tried to contact those inside the building. Neighbors said they saw snipers on nearby rooftops. Around 11:00 a.m., the police took Uscamayta out unharmed, shirtless and handcuffed.

Bank of America employee Juan Uscamayta is removed from the bank handcuffed and guarded by specialized agents of the FBI's rapid action squad.

What was appropriate in cases like this was to collect information on the main suspect, who was Juan Uscamayta. Interviews with the suspect's closest acquaintances began.

Hugo Núñez, a friend of Uscamayta, since they were studying at South Miami High School, said that he was a responsible young man who had recently been promoted in the bank.

"I can't believe Juan is involved in something like that," Núñez told El Nuevo Herald, Florida's leading newspaper. He is a victim of all this. Núñez added that Uscamayta's sister, Karla, also works at another Bank of America branch. Uscamayta's twin, Monica, preferred not to speak to the press or the Investigators.

On Thursday night, Núñez added, Uscamayta's mother, Gladys, was on duty at the hospital where she works.

Gladys, who was wearing a nurse's uniform, also did not speak to the press, only receiving Núñez, in the Nob Hill apartment, which was also cordoned off by the police in search of evidence. Milton Chávez, another friend of Juan Uscamayta's, since high school, said he was studious and had never been in trouble with the law. I am worried about what has happened to John, so I have come to visit his family.

The interviews that were conducted with different people talked about the personality and morals of the young cashier; We had to continue the investigation until we got to where the real criminals were.

The important thing now was to find the young man's car where some evidence could be obtained that would shed light on the case and alert the public about the dangerous criminals who carried high-caliber weapons.

The security agencies in coordination with the insurance company offered a reward. These are things that help a little when acts of this nature happen.

"The FBI is offering a $50,000.00 reward for any information leading to an arrest of those responsible."

Juan Uscamayta, after being questioned by the FBI for several hours, was declared a victim. A search was ordered for the criminals who fled in the red car, which was later found parked in an apartment complex a few blocks from the Bank, the FBI spokesman said. The car was discovered at 1:00 p.m. that same Friday, due precautions were taken before entering it for fear that there was an explosive inside.

The car was towed to an undisclosed location for processing, he said, according to Orihuela, an FBI executive, the car showed that its owner was a humble person.

George, Uscamayta's older brother, told reporters outside the family's Nob Hill apartment in Kendall on Saturday that his brother would sleep in and not talk to them. He added that his brother would make a statement in a few days.

According to police, there were many unanswered questions. At the end of the day, the circumstances surrounding the bank robbery were unclear; The bomb was fake, the kidnappers took a lot of money, the ATM was interrogated for more than 15 hours. On Saturday afternoon, three FBI agents dressed in T-shirts and carrying handguns and badges arrived at the Uscamayta family's apartment

The FBI spokeswoman confirmed that the vest contained explosive elements, they were still analyzing the device. The fact that Juan had recently been promoted and that he had been given a set of keys to open the door of the bank stood out. The keys were not discovered by the thieves; Juan never mentioned to them that he had them and said in his interview with the police that he did not talk about the keys because he thought that, if the thieves did not have that information, he could get out of the matter and prevent them from taking the money.

This fact ruled out some clues since the assailants only had information obtained with the monitoring and surveillance they made to Juan, but they did not know about the changes they had made, such as the promotion and the set of keys that the manager had given him. This ruled out the possibility that there was an accomplice inside the bank.

Our investigation indicated that the thieves we were pursuing had pulled off another masterstroke by painstakingly planning to leave the authorities accusing an innocent man.

Our primary objective was to obtain evidence that would show the FBI or the Prosecutor's Office that our client, Dante Antonio Hank, was innocent of the charges against him. We had to be very careful because these thieves are career criminals who, while they are in prison, dedicate themselves to preparing to commit crimes again and because they have more experience and time to plan, they do it perfectly.

This case had become complicated due to the intelligence of the criminal who led this small but effective gang of robbers. The only way forward was to take up the case of the accusation against Dante Antonio Hank.

"Research is what I do when I don't know what I'm doing."

Wernher Von Braun

10

ON THE TRAIL OF THE ASSAILANTS

We focused on Digna Sandoval; her restaurant was still the point that would take us where we wanted to be if we continued to pay attention to surveillance. We talked to John, the undercover agent we had working in the parking lot.

-We need you to take a little more risk in this case.

-Tell me what the next step is.

-Try to be close to the daughter, because she will take you to the father.

-Do you want me to make her fall in love?

-I don't think it's a good idea.

-An employee told me that the boss slept with a young man who came to work about two weeks ago.

-How did she know?

-The dishwasher was in the kitchen doing his job, my friend smoked a cigarette under one of the tables to snack on the salads, Digna arrived at that moment and thought she was alone with the young man who was peeling some potatoes that were needed for the next day.

-What happened?

-It was three in the morning and almost all the employees had left, Digna looked down the corridor and as she saw no one, she said to the young man:

-Leave that for tomorrow, it's too late. Are you planning to stay overnight here?

-I like to leave everything clean and ready for the next day

-We'll do something.

-Tell me what I should do.

-Tonight, I want you to stay at my house, I need you to help me move some furniture tomorrow, before I come to work."

-As you say, boss.

-We'll take a bottle of wine home, maybe we'll come up with something good.

-The young man did not answer, he turned red because he knew that his partner was under the table and listened to the boss's proposal. The next day, she arrived at about 5:00 in the afternoon with the new employee whom we all looked at and thought was lucky to have taken the boss.

It wasn't a bad idea to have an investigator sleep with this elusive woman, but I didn't want to risk our spy so much, so I came up with a different strategy that could give us the same results.

-I want you to stick to Digna, as much as you can, avoid falling in love with her, but if you see an opportunity don't miss it; Take it very carefully because if those people find out your intentions, they could kill you.

-Are they so dangerous?

-More than you can imagine.

I left the way open for John to deal with the matter at his discretion; It is very difficult to order an investigator who is on a knife's edge, to do things that can cause death for doing a job that could well wait because in the end, all criminals fall involved in their own nets. Seven days passed without any news until one night Digna's father arrived, with his partners in a Land Rover car, black LRX series, which he parked in the VIP area.

-Mr. Martinez, a car driven by the boss's father has just arrived, he is accompanied by three people, including a woman.

-Try to be cautious, I don't want you to risk too much, I'm on my way, I'll be around in about fifteen minutes."

In the car that John parked, there were: Diego Sandoval, who was driving, Carmen Loaiza, Jerry Corona and his half-brother, Sanfor Carpí.

I sped out, I wanted to have these thugs in my photos again for when I presented the evidence to the FBI. It was 1:30 in the morning, a light drizzle was falling, which made the night cold, gloomy and with little traffic, which made it difficult to follow up on the suspects. John, inside the premises, tried to prick up his ears to hear what the diners were talking about inside the VIP lounge that had been reserved for this special dinner.

I had to enter that room as I pleased. John was looking for the opportunity to sneak in, he was near the door waiting for his turn when he saw Digna coming, with two containers of ice that he would put in the middle of the table where the guests shared.

That was John's opportunity to enter where only Digna, the cook and Carmen, who served Diego Sandoval and his companions, the dishes prepared especially for the occasion, were allowed to enter.

John took the ice, emptied it into a bucket to go to the forbidden door, entered without paying attention to the gazes of those people. The conversation stopped for a few seconds, then the boss spoke again, calling the attention of those present.

-Who gave you permission to enter this meeting?

The gathered looked towards the corner where John was placing the bucket full of ice so that they could help themselves if they needed it, he sat up and asked:

-Do you mean me, sir?

-Yes, why did you enter here?

-I work in the restaurant, sir.

-That doesn't give you the right to listen to our conversations.

-I am not doing such a thing, sir.

-I want you to tell me what the fuck you're doing inside this room?

Everyone expected a tragic outcome in that situation that John had gotten himself into who, without stopping, challenged the man who had the power to physically abuse him if he felt like it.

"I noticed that Miss Digna came in with two small ice containers and I thought that if she had a bucket with all the ice, she wouldn't have to stop every now and then to go to the kitchen in search of more ice.

-Daughter, what is this man doing in your restaurant?

-Work in the parking lot.

-Can someone explain to me what the fuck this intruder is doing here?

-Father, calm down.

-I asked you a question!

The woman realized that if she did not act cautiously someone would get hurt from that episode, she had to act immediately without allowing things to get out of control.

-John!

-Yes, miss

-Thank you for your help, but it is better that you continue at your stall in front of the premises so that you can attend to the customers who arrive, if someone comes at this time.

-Okay, miss.

Without wasting time, the young man left the room like lightning; Digna's father got up from his seat.

-I don't like that young man

-Father, you always see visions.

-Thanks to my precautions, we are gathered together to celebrate in this room.

-Sit down, father, if you want to say goodbye.

The man gave her an approving look that left the matter settled, the guests and the hostess hurried to move the cutlery, bring the plates closer and taste the drink to alleviate the situation.

John, back in the parking lot, dialed my phone.

"Sir, those people are more dangerous than I thought.

"What happened?"

John, he told me what had happened; I realized that the young man had not measured the consequences, and I made the necessary clarifications.

-You have to get rid of your cell phone, listen to me carefully; I will pass in front of the restaurant where you are, have your phone in your hands when I approach, I will pretend that I am lost and I will ask you for an address, you take advantage and drop the phone inside my car; I'll take the device with me.

-That is not necessary.

-You don't know what you're doing, son!

-What did he say?

-If you don't do what I say, you're fired!

What the fuck have I gotten myself into, I don't understand anything!

I stopped my car in front of the store, John, he was approaching with a stupid smile, he approached the right door of my Mercedes Benz, I lowered the window to tell him.

-When they ask you about the phone, tell them that you don't have any.

-I can't do that, I'd be lying, everyone here knows that I have a phone.

-Do as I tell you, I'm about to have a heart attack.

I was aware that John had no experience, but if I didn't follow a direct order when it was given, I could cause a catastrophe within my organization. I left the area, turned the corner to the right and came back a few minutes later. I placed myself in the same place where I was before and refocused my camera so that when the diners left, I could take them together in the photo.

It was 2:45 in the morning when I called several associates of my group to mislead the genius of organized crime Diego Sandoval, I placed them in a row behind and in front of my car so that they would not see a single car in front of the restaurant. The clock read 3:10 a.m. when the subjects began to leave.

First came the man of color, Jerry Corona, who looked in all directions and entered again the place that looked alone and uninhabited at that time of the morning; then they all left in a group, except Jerry Corona.

The man who directed looked everywhere, we had to admit that he did his job very well; he sensed danger, he was an individual with a lot of experience; even though she knew that he was a criminal, she felt a certain admiration for him. These are the kinds of challenges I like to face as I am forced to work as smart as possible.

Diego Sandoval approached his daughter and said:

-Where is the young man who came into our meeting?

-Daddy, leave that!

Digna replied, trying to forget the situation.

-I just want to ask you one thing.

The woman, knowing who her father was, immediately called John, who tried to hide until the danger disappeared, but he had no other option, he had to show his face.

-Tell me, miss.

-My father wants to ask you something.

-Tell me, sir.

-Give me your cell phone, I want to check it to clear up any doubts.

-I don't have a cell phone, sir.

Diego Sandoval knew that he was at a disadvantage; he saw all those cars parked in front of his daughter's business and in fractions of a second he deduced that the boy was not alone in this and that the FBI could be on his heels.

Diego thought he had to disappear as soon as possible; he kissed his daughter goodbye, asking her to say goodbye to John first.

-Fire that wretches immediately, he's a federal.

-Yes, father, go with God.

The super leader did not say a single word, neither did his daughter, she limited herself to saying goodbye to her guests to enter her restaurant again; She was upset about the unpleasant time she had gone through. John was colder than the early morning, inside he blessed me for my decision to go and take his cell phone. If this man had seen the names and phone numbers in his contact list, John would surely be a dead man.

A few minutes after that encounter with reality occurred, John was called by the owner of the restaurant to her offices to talk to him about matters of interest.

-John, everything has a fix in life.

-Tell me, miss.

-Open that briefcase.

When the young man opened the briefcase, he realized that there was something there that he had never seen in his life; It was full of dollars in $100.00 and $50.00 bills.

-What is this?

-In that briefcase there are two million dollars that you can take with you, they are yours.

-She's going crazy!

-Just tell me the truth and you're rich, this will be between you and me.

-What are you talking about?

-Are you federal?

-No!

-Do you work with the law?

-Miss!

-Just answer, if you tell the truth you can keep the money, I have much more than that, but I want peace of mind.

-Miss, you know me, I don't know why they doubt me.

-We will do something, I will dial your phone if it rings or someone answers it, that man behind you will shoot you with his pistol that will not make much noise because it has a silencer.

The man came out of hiding, John knew him, his name was often mentioned in the underworld, he was the murderer, the black man, Jerry Corona.

John was at a crossroads, if I answered, his life was worth nothing and if I didn't it was in their hands. The woman dialed the phone, I could see on the screen that someone was trying to communicate with John, I never thought about what was happening, but I did sense that something strange was happening in there; he suspected that the black Jerry Corona had stayed inside the restaurant for some special reason, because he did not go out with the others.

When no one answered, the woman continued with her interrogation.

-Why did you lie to my father?

-I never did such a thing, miss!

-You told him you didn't have a phone.

-It's the truth!

-You think I'm stupid, where do you think I was calling?

-Ask everyone, I didn't bring a phone today because it fell in the bathtub and hurt me. Digna Sandoval, stared at the black Jerry Corona, the seconds were eternal. John thought that his death was certain, he had underestimated those people and he did not believe what his boss, researcher Martínez, told him.

-What is your opinion, Jerry?

-It's better to die, so we can get rid of doubts.

-They're crazy!

The poor boy peed on his pants, his urine running between his legs soaked his socks and shoes. Digna realized the fear that the young man was feeling and confronted him with a few soft words.

-You owe me your life, if I ever hear you say anything about what happened here, I'll send black Jerry to fulfill his wish to kill you.

-I'll never say anything, I promise.

-Deal done, now get out of my restaurant.

He was a little relieved to have been saved from death, but he felt a terrible fear, something he had never felt before. He came out without saying a single word, took his car, stepped on the accelerator to the bottom and left the area screaming tires.

Although I didn't have details, I realized that John was up against the wall, but more importantly, he was out of imminent danger now. One of my partners who was in the line of parked cars followed him a short distance. John took the main highway at high-speed believing that whoever was following him was one of the bad guys, my partner called me to inform me; that he was laughing to death from what I supposed John was thinking.

The black Jerry Corona, left with Diego Sandoval's daughter, in a car that I did not want to follow because they would detect me immediately due to the little traffic that was in the streets at that time. We left the danger zone at 5:20 in the morning.

In my work there is no start or end time, which is sometimes good; The next day I woke up at 9:00 p.m. because my biological clock had broken down because of the vigilance of the night before. When I woke up, the first thing I did was contact Alex, to let her know what was going on.

-I want you to track down John, we need to talk to him.

-They told me part of what happened last night, get up because it is time to act.

-I'm old and tired, I don't have your energy.

-You make yourself feel sorry and then you give us lectures on survival or resistance.

-Remember that the art of deception is only practiced by those who want to know the truth.

-Stop cheap philosophy, get out of bed, I'll wait for you with John, in an hour in our office.

-No, we'd better go eat something good because I'm starving, I have to recharge my batteries.

-Okay, see you in the usual restaurant.

I'm not a big fan of eating red meat, but in this restaurant the specialty was a variety of salads with all kinds of meats. They put a red lid on one side and green on the other, when you want the servants with different meats to parade in front of your table, you turn the green lid, if you want to stop you turn it red.

After eating like a hungry lion, they bring you another dessert party, I recommend the papaya, milky or bomb fruit cream or whatever you want to call it, this is to die of pleasure.

I arrived at the restaurant where Alex and the frightened John were eating, after greeting them I began to find out what happened that electrifying rainy night in the restaurant of Diego Sandoval's daughter.

-I didn't listen to him when he warned me that those people were dangerous. John said.

-One thing you must be very clear, when I give you an order you have to comply with it.

-Remember, I'm new to this.

-An oversight can cost you your life in this job.

-There is something that has taken away hours of sleep.

-What is it?

-How did I know that that woman's father would ask me for my phone?

-To catch a criminal, you have to think like him and take a step ahead of his actions, otherwise he will win the game.

-You do know how to work in these matters, for a moment I came to think that you had divine powers.

-That's called experience!

"I thought you were a sorcerer.

-What was it that gave you away?

-I decided to act and they didn't buy the story.

-Did you manage to hear anything they were saying?

-I heard Miss Digna's father say, *'I'm thinking about how to get back to that bank.'*

-The colored man who almost murdered me said, "*I don't think you're crazy.*

-In addition, Diego Sandoval, who led the table said:

-I'll rob that bank again

-That man is very intelligent.

-I don't think he bought the story.

-They suspected you were an FBI agent.

-It's possible.

-What saved your life was that Digna went out to the front and saw several cars with people inside them, she knew that, if you were really an

FBI agent and you didn't get out of your job alive, the others who were watching would eat her alive before escaping.

-Because of the doubt they had, those wretches did not pull the trigger.

"You have to take care of yourself because if they find out that you work for me, you will be a dead man; You are a witness against them, and because they do not know what you saw or heard, they will walk after your head like mad dogs.

- Don't freak out, boss.

-It's serious, you have to take care of yourself.

I realized that my assistant Alex was not speaking, he was thinking about something he could not guess. When a woman analyzes an issue related to her or her family, which in this case was us, you have to pay attention.

-Chief, I think those degenerate murderers will rob the Bank of America again.

-They can't take so many risks.

-These criminals are professionals; they will look for a way to do it just to prove to the FBI that they are shit.

-I don't share your opinion, but it has a bit of logic.

The dinner ended late, we talked for a long time and then we left satisfied with the progress we had made.

The next day I arrived at my office at about 11:00 in the morning when I entered my office, the troubled John, he was sweaty and red as if he had come out of a sauna bath.

-Boss, I have the impression that when I was coming, two cars are following me

-I can't believe you brought them here without first misleading them.

-When he was arriving, I lost sight of him.

-Shit, now you really have to take care of yourself, friend!

-What does "Boss mean?"

-If those people put surveillance on you and followed you, they will realize that you work for me and that you are an important piece of the puzzle that I am putting together.

-Now I'm really screwed!

-We will look for a solution.

-What damn trouble am I in?

-Don't worry, my friend, don't lose control, if you do, you'll be easy prey for them.

Things were getting more and more dangerous; if John had allowed himself to be followed to the office we were in a tremendous predicament.

A call came in like any other, someone was asking for John, who was in my office at the time.

The secretary came in and said:

-Call for John on line three

The young man jumped out of his seat to answer; I quickly stopped his hand and said:

-Look for the recorder before picking up the phone.

-For what?

-For your sake, I have to fire you after you answer that call.

-What did I do now?

-Find the recorder and hurry up, if the person on the line is smart, he will realize that you are preparing to record it.

The young man looked at me suspiciously, he didn't know why I had acted like that. I was absolutely sure that things would change after I picked up the phone. The device was turned on to record the conversation; We heard a woman's voice say:

-John!

-Yes.

-I gave you the opportunity to take two million dollars and you didn't.

-Miss Digna!

-You swore to me that you did not work for the law.

-That is the truth

-Where are you now, in a church?

-It is a law firm; you know that I study criminal justice.

-You work for a rat named Angel Martinez.

-Jesus Christ!

-Don't be surprised, we know everything about you.

-I am not committing any crime.

-Of that we are sure, what you can never stop is the promise that Jerry made you.

-I really don't remember it.

-Wait a minute.

There was a pause in the conversation, the person who was on the line was surely passing the phone to another individual; he suspected it was the colored man named Jerry. When we felt the breathing of the person who returned to the phone, we heard a man's voice say:

-John!

-Say.

-Do you think I can trust you?

-Who's speaking?

-You know well that I am your little friend Jerry.

"Mr. Jerry, I don't have any friends who start a conversation by pointing at the heads of people with guns with silencers.

"Play the miserable little man, when I put my hands on you not even your mother will recognize you."

The call was cut off by those who made the death threat. We couldn't act lightly, we had to protect the naïve John, against these murderers.

We tracked down the FBI special agent and called an emergency meeting introducing young John as a victim to be protected.

The intelligence services that were in charge of the protection of witnesses in the United States had to start their work. One of our attorneys, who would represent our employee, arranged for a representative of the federal government and the prosecution to be present at the meeting.

We arrived at the FBI offices, with the intention that our man would be granted all the guarantees that correspond to an American citizen who requires protection. We presented the evidence we had to prove that John was a target of the assailants. I started the conversation to gain an advantage.

If possible, I would like this meeting to be divided into two parts

The prosecutor representing the government was concerned about my position.

-What two things are we going to talk about?

"We will deal with the case of John, who is present here, and the injustice you are committing with another young man who is in prison while innocent.

"That's out of place, I didn't come here to discuss anyone's innocence.

"You are the only one who does not know why you came to this meeting.

Tempers were heating up in a meeting that was just beginning, but my intention was precisely that; I wanted it to come to light that they, those who represented justice in the United States, had a man imprisoned just for filling out statistics and not for doing justice.

FBI Special Agent Manuel Fernandez intervened to strengthen my purpose.

-The best thing for everyone is that we calm down, in short, this is a meeting between friends; here we are all pursuing the same thing. After we are calm, I want Researcher Martínez to tell us in detail what those two situations that we would deal with in this meeting are.

I was giving myself the opportunity to tell the feds that my client, young Dante Antonio Hank, was one of the many innocents who were in the overcrowded prisons of the United States.

-A young man who may be the age of one of our children is rotting in a prison because the evidence of his case was not studied in depth.

FBI agent Manuel Fernández had allowed me to bring out my point of view, then he took the floor to define the process that we would carry out in that meeting.

Mr. Martinez, we thank you for your concern. You and all of you gathered in this room know that the FBI is an institution that seeks the cleanliness and truth of every case that is considered a crime within our country. Today we are gathered to deal only with the case of death threats to John, who as an informant of the investigator Martínez, has been threatened with death by some dangerous murderers whom we want to catch.

My friend Manuel Fernández, had put things back in their place with the speech he gave I felt immense satisfaction when this man showed that my research was yielding good results. Although he did not say it clearly, his insinuations made me think that he would have the opportunity to prove that my client, Dante Hank's son, was innocent of all the charges against him.

We gave the recording of the death threat that we had taken from Diego Sandoval's daughter who, by coincidences of life, had been shot several years ago, inside a bank by agent Manuel Fernández, who today was a supervisor within the FBI. John gave his statement; the FBI took the notes for the report they would make to the State Department.

124

"The jury is made up of twelve people chosen to decide who has the best lawyer."

Robert Frost

11

A PROTECTED WITNESS

In 1929 the Italian mafias had the United States in a state of upheaval because of the work carried out by criminal organizations. Al Capone and Lucky Luciano, its main leaders, filled the streets of the most important states of the American nation with blood and corpses.

These criminals called themselves "The Black Hand" and created what was called: "The Code of Silence".

These titles or slogans were very much taken into account by ordinary citizens; anyone who spoke to the police would be liquidated. By 1946 the situation was beyond the control of the authorities; The criminals sent messages to the different detachments of a terrified society that kept silent and hindered any type of investigation that arose as a result of the multiple murders and criminal acts perpetrated in the different cities. The collaboration that the authorities received from the community was nil.

To counteract this situation, they wanted to organize what the agencies called by various names: Witness Safety Program, Witness Relocation Program, or Witness Protection Program. This was due to the struggle that has always existed between the different agencies that fight crime in the United States, as they never agree.

Congress warned that the country was taking a very dangerous course, when a new ingredient contributed by criminal organizations entered the scene with overwhelming force; it was an excessively lucrative activity.

The trafficking of drugs such as methamphetamine and other stimulants had an important and growing market despite the partial opposition of the old guard of crime, represented by traditional mobsters who did not want to get involved in the new business. One of the first arrests made was that of mobster Pete Casella. In 1959 Casella was sentenced to fifteen years in prison.

This fact proved the former capos right who did not want to venture into drug trafficking, but for the mafias the damage was already done; Federal agencies had propagated that the Italians, in addition to their businesses of extortion, robbery and murder, were starting a new illicit activity, drug trafficking.

Attorney General Robert Kennedy set about strengthening and institutionalizing the Witness Protection Program, with the aim of using it as a weapon against organized crime. The Department of Justice was looking for a way to guarantee the safety of witnesses and found in the prosecutor a very valuable ally.

The Program was responsible for relocating and changing the identity of witnesses. This Program had $11,000,000.00 million dollars from the government budget and 200 agents, who were in charge of protecting about 600 criminals of the worst kind, but who had taken advantage of the protection of the federal government.

This Program had some restrictions that were put on the table in the agreement that John made with the Miami prosecutors. Following the information that the young man and our investigation department provided to the security services, John's lawyer said:

-If there is an agreement at this time, we are ready to sign.

"Before we make any agreement, I want to know if we are really interested in what your client is going to tell us in court.

The prosecutor continued in his position of not giving anything in exchange for something that did not interest him.

Let me remind you that without a witness there can be no trial or conviction and without protection there will be no witness.

"I have to consult your request with the State Department in Washington, I will give you a written response in a week," replied the prosecutor.

John's lawyer knew that he had to get a written and signed document from the prosecutor because otherwise we would have nothing in the immediate future.

The prosecutor took the floor again and said:

-We will draft a provisional agreement that we will present in Washington, if it is approved, we do not have to meet again to waste valuable time that we could use in other activities.

"John's defense agrees.

-These are the terms: The witness will never have communication with his relatives again, he will not be able to make contacts with his old friends, he will be sent to an undetermined place and no one will know his whereabouts, every document he possesses will be changed, we will give him a short time to choose a name, at that time he will be fingerprinted and he will have a new birth certificate and a new identification. Any message you want to send to him, Mr. Attorney and also us, will be through a security system controlled by the Witness Protection Program. No federal agency will know his whereabouts, he will be given $3,000,000 dollars for his maintenance for a while, until he stabilizes his economic situation with a decent job and is given to him

$9,000.00 thousand dollars to buy a car for personal use.

The prosecutor paused to gather momentum and conclude his work, according to the criteria of the American bureaucrats in Washington.

I didn't want to leave anything to chance, the terms had to be clear enough for the parties to understand that if there was any fault everything would be canceled immediately. The prosecutor continued:

-Finally, if you commit an infraction of the provisions of this agreement, your child support payments will be canceled and you can be arrested until all the processes that we will initiate against organized crime are finished, which we can extend for a long time.

All the points of the U.S. witness protection program were put in that document. With the Feds it is much better to have everything in writing because the bureaucracy can leave it on the street if it does not have something to support any agreement with the Federal Government.

"It is better to risk saving a guilty person than to condemn an innocent person."

Voltaire

12

THEY HAVE DONE IT AGAIN

The job we gave young John had brought his death sentence or his disappearance, knowing of his whereabouts only to the United States Witness Protection Program. The boy had very good intentions, but that doesn't buy you a living, that was one of the reasons why I decided to take him out of the environment until everything returned to normal.

The situation was calm when one morning my assistant Alex arrived at my desk with a nervous breakdown.

-They repeated it.

-What happened?

-The Bank of America was robbed again.

"It can't be true!"

At the moment the area is surrounded by an army of police who cannot believe what happened there.

Special operations officers in front of the banking institution robbed for the second time in a course of 17 days in Miami, Florida, United States.

A man in his 20s, sportily dressed in a light-colored cap, a purple T-shirt and an animal painted on his attire, approached the bench at

9:50 a.m. on October 11, 2010, he stopped for a few moments at the front of the building, looked around and pushed open the front door of the bank, lined up behind about five people who were waiting their turn to do their banking transactions.

When it was his turn, in front of the station of cashier number three, he smiled and handed him a note that said:

"You have three minutes to fill this bag of money for me, if you sound the alarm I will shoot you, if you tell the guard I will shoot you, if you want to die today, I will shoot you"

The individual retreated a few steps back so that the cashier could see the bundle he had in his waist covered with the T-shirt he was wearing, when the cashier surreptitiously handed him the money, the thief told him:

"At the moment, there are seven people in the waiting line, you won't know which of them will shoot you, if he sees that you make a signal to the security guard or if you hear a siren when I'm leaving."

"Don't worry, sir, I swear I won't do anything!"

The assailant left with his bag full of dollars without arousing suspicion. The cashier, in addition to being nervous, was undecided about what to do at that moment, for fear that one of the people who were in line would shoot her in the head; This gave the thief enough time to disappear walking and enter a supermarket to change clothes and thus not be chased. He vanished with a large sum of money, once again these intrepid assailants had struck a great blow.

The director of the FBI in Miami was furious about what was happening in his community. Actions like these left their bodies in a bad light as investigators or hunters of bank robbers. This super-agent who led a corps of more than 750 men asked for a meeting with the group supervisors to tell him the following:

This morning, I received a call from the Attorney General of the Nation to ask me about what is happening in my community. I will not take this pressure because of you who do not do your job well.

I want you to know that I will be breathing behind your neck if possible so that you can do things right.

I want results, I want those sons of bitches who are exhausting my patience. My ulcer is bleeding, that wretch Diego Sandoval must fall as soon as possible; You know he's a smart and careful criminal, I don't want you to be the laughingstock of our competitors, I want results, now!

The FBI chief spoke without leaving a single doubt as to what was required to catch the thief who had him losing sleep. The supervisors of areas and teams would have to put on their pants to activate the network of informants that the FBI has, within their community and thus obtain the clues to find the base of operations of the damn criminal named Diego Sandoval.

"He who flees from judgment confesses the crime".

Seneca

13

THE SMALL DETAILS OF AN INVESTIGATION

When you're doing research work and see all roads closed, the advice I always give is to go back to square one and analyze every step you took to see where the possible solution is.

I dressed in my best suit and went to spend a day with my client's son, who was in the Federal Prison in Miami.

Dante Antonio Hank looked more relaxed than the first day I visited. A few days were enough to realize that the only thing he could do was to be patient; He gave me a big hug and a smile; Then we start the conversation:

"I thought he had forgotten about me.

"You thought you were bad, friend!"

-How are things?

-Every day better, I'm discovering the conspiracy that those murderous sons of bitches wove against you.

-I read in the newspapers that the Bank of America was robbed again

-Yes, things are happening that only God knows.

-When will you have a solution to the case?

"It's not that easy!"

-I have full confidence in what he is doing.

-I want to go back to what we talked about earlier.

"I'm not going anywhere, tell me what you want to know, and I'll answer you truthfully, in this situation I have nothing to lose."

My client was desperate, but in control of his actions; the prison tames even the most ferocious wolves; Being incarcerated is a punishment I don't wish on anyone. I began to inquire again about the small details of the case that was now stalled, and I did not know where to continue.

-When you arrived at the university on the day of the assault, it was 8:00 in the morning, the guard swears that you left through the door at 8:30, here is a small and significant detail that I made the security guard sign when I interviewed him.

-What is that detail?

-According to the guard, when you entered the University, he remembers the plaid shirt you were wearing that day, because it looked like one, he has.

-What does that have to do with the case?

-The robber carried out the robbery with a red shirt, which he wanted to compare with the photo found in your car.

-What shirt were you wearing on the day of the robbery?

"Since you didn't stop at the door, the guard doesn't remember if you had a plaid shirt.

-Good observation.

-I studied all the videos of the University and found images of you entering the bathrooms, at 8:50 in the morning.

"Yes, now I remember that I was in the bathroom!"

-If you were inside the University, who was driving your car at that time?

"Shit, now this has become tangled, Mr. Martinez!"

-I saw you leaving the bathrooms of the University at 9:05 in the morning.

- How is it possible that you are in two places at the same time?

"Tomorrow I will have a meeting with the feds, if they don't get you out of jail and drop all the charges, I will make a fuss in all the media in the world.

"Mr. Martinez!"

-Yes!

"Perfection is a wonderful virtue that weighs so heavily that man cannot cope with it.

-I don't understand your philosophy.

-I think I will go free because of the perfection of your analyses.

"Don't hesitate, my friend, you'll be free in a few hours!"

I went to court for a hearing with the judge in his office. When the magistrate saw all the evidence he only said:

In my profession you never know when you will receive an unpredictable lesson.

The young Dante Antonio Hank was released, I follow in the footsteps of this gang of criminals who today have become the most important persecuted by the authorities of
the United States.

"When I catch it, I'll write the second part"

Ángel Martínez

"We live in a society that is deeply dependent on science and technology and in which no one knows anything about these issues. This is a sure formula for disaster."

Carl Sagan

(1934 - 1996) was an American astrophysicist, astronomer and science communicator who, for decades, dedicated himself to explaining in a simple way all the mysteries surrounding the cosmos.

THE MEANING OF THIS WORK.

IDENTITY THEFT: A GLOBAL PROBLEM

What is identity theft?

Identity theft is any kind of fraud that results in the loss of personal data, such as passwords, usernames, banking information, or credit card numbers.

Online identity theft is sometimes referred to as spoofing.

Identity theft is not new. Thieves have always found ways to illegally appropriate personal information through deception (also known as social engineering), stealing mail from mailboxes, and even going through trash cans. Now that identity theft has moved online, criminals can trick a larger number of people, making it much more profitable.

The Internet has revolutionized the way we communicate with the people around us, and, in many cases, it has served as a bridge to establish new professional contacts or connect with people with common hobbies or concerns. Social networks are an instrument with which many people stay in touch with their friends, look for a job or share their photos or videos, however, in the face of this enormous flow of personal data that travels through the network, we find that there are people with not very good intentions who will try to access this data to trade with them or, in some cases, impersonate our identity.

It may seem exaggerated, but according to the European observatory, 4% of European Union citizens were victims of personal data theft and/or identity theft, a figure that increases in the cases of Spain and Bulgaria with 7% of Internet users in these countries. In fact, to take into account the seriousness of the situation, 3% of European Internet users suffered financial losses due to fraudulent use of their credit card or phishing attacks (with Latvia leading the way with 8% of its Internet users).

Let's think that our profiles on Facebook and Twitter, in some way, are also our calling card and, in the wrong hands, could cause great damage to our reputation; That is why we must take extreme precautions to prevent this from happening and, if we are unfortunate enough to be a victim of identity theft, act quickly to mitigate the damage caused and tackle the problem as soon as possible.

What is identity theft?

Identity theft consists of unauthorized access to one of our profiles, our email account or our online banking account, that is, when someone gets our username and password in a service or is able to find out our password or the answer to the "secret question".

Identity theft is much older than social media, in fact, it happened if someone's ID or credit card was stolen and, for example, purchases were made in their name. However, the widespread use of online services has led to the emergence of digital identity theft, whether to spy on what someone does/says, smear their name, impersonate them or steal confidential data.

How can access to our account be stolen?

A mistake, for example, can lead to unauthorized access to one of our accounts. Forgetfulness? Yes, for example, leaving us logged in to a shared computer or leaving our computer with open sessions in the browser and letting someone use it (without our supervision), actions that we do not give importance to but that involve the exposure of our accounts to a third party.

But, perhaps, the greatest risk is in ourselves. A bad personal password policy can be a problem for the preservation of our digital identity. Using the same password on all web services that we're registered for is a big risk, basically, because if you compromise one, they all are. This is one of the most common mistakes that, together with sharing the password with friends and/or family, writing down the password in the notes of the mobile phone or on a piece of paper that we keep in the wallet and putting an obvious in the answer to the "secret questions" are bad practices that compromise our data. Making it difficult for these "friends of the alien 2.0" is in our hands and the password is something that we define ourselves.

How can we realize?

Unfortunately, identity theft is detected reactively, that is, we find out when it has happened, and we have noticed some of its effects.

Effects?

Yes, let's imagine that one day we try to access our email account or our Facebook profile and no matter how much we repeat the password, it appears invalid. We try to recover the password through the secret question, but we are not able to find the correct answer either; Shortly after, one of our friends calls us to ask us about an off-color post we have made on Facebook and when we go to the ATM we find a purchase, paid through PayPal, that we have not made.

Although it may seem like a nightmare or the script of a TV movie, it is something that could and does happen. Normally the user finds out after it has happened and, in cases of phishing or theft of identity documents, victims have found themselves on lists of defaulters for non-payment of invoices for purchases that they never made. In the world of social networks, it could also cost us some upset because, if someone entered our LinkedIn account and left an unfriendly message to our CEO, they would probably not be too amused.

How to act in the event of identity theft?

If we have been a victim of identity theft or suspect that something is not working well, we must act quickly, but without losing our calm.

If we still have access to the service, that is, our credentials are still valid, it is time to change the passwords of all the services to one that does not keep a similar pattern and that, in addition, does not contain strings of significant characters (surnames, first names, cities, dates of birth, etc.). On the downside, it would be the most favorable scenario since we could tackle the problem autonomously, but it is good to take a look at our accounts to review the publications made. In fact, we should do this way if our password is exposed for any reason (even if there are no signs of theft or impersonation).

In the worst-case scenario, we could be without access to our email account and/or any of our social profiles. In such a case, we have to remain calm and address the problem on two fronts: regain control of our accounts and bring the case to the attention of the authorities.

In order to regain control of our accounts, practically all services have published a procedure that regulates how to contact those responsible for the service to report the loss of control of our account, request a temporary suspension of its activity or regain control of it.

In addition, to avoid being held responsible for what they do or publish from our profiles (third-party complaints, blacklisting, etc.) we must inform the authorities of what has happened.**How can we be forewarned?**

Although no one is free from being a victim of identity theft, it is true that we can make it a little more complicated for those who try to access our data, simply by following some guidelines that will help us to be better protected:

Never use the same password in all the services in which we are registered and, in addition, do not use simple passwords that are easily associated with us (dates of birth, names, surnames, pets, etc.).

Do not share the access password with anyone and change it after a reasonable time, at least three months a year and never repeat it as if it were a sequence.

On shared or publicly used computers, use anonymous browsing mode or empty cache, history, passwords, and saved forms.

Pay attention to the websites we usually access to see if they have undergone any substantial changes or, in the case of electronic banking, do not appear as secure sites.
Do not leave your computer unattended, unlocked and with open sessions.

Never send passwords by email. Web services such as Facebook or Twitter, or electronic banking, will never ask us by email to send them the password and, if we receive an email like this, it is probably a *phishing attempt.*

In conclusion, we must try not to expose more data than necessary not only on social networks, to commercial agents, who call us on the phone and to strangers who for some reason want to have data on our identity.

A last request protects your minor children, the care that parents should have about the activities that their children carry out, both on social networks and outside the home, is never extreme.

What are the most common types of identity theft?
Back in 2019, the Consumer Sentinel Network, which is part of the U.S. Federal Trade Commission (FTC), received more than 3.2 million fraud complaints. Identity theft was the top category, accounting for 20.3% of reported cases, with more reports being filed related to identity theft and fraudulent charges, in all their various forms, than any other type of complaint, including imposter scams and phone and mobile services.

The 3 Most Common Types of Identity Theft
- Credit card fraud
- Loan or rental fraud
- Phone or utility fraud

Interestingly, the age group most affected by identity theft is younger people, who report losing money to fraud more often than older people, while older people tend to lose a higher amount of money on average.

It doesn't matter the age group. Anyone is at risk of becoming a victim of a form of identity theft.

Type of identity theft #1:
Credit card fraud

Credit card fraud was already at the top of the list for identity theft complaints in 2019. The FTC received more than 271,000 complaints from people who said their information was misused in an existing account or used to open a new credit card account.

The number of new fraudulent accounts opened in 2019 was 246,763, an increase of 88% from the previous year. On the other hand, the number of fraud complaints on existing accounts decreased by 4% to 31,022.

However, credit card fraud far exceeds the number of identity-related reports compared to any other type.

Examples of credit card identity theft

Credit card fraud can occur in many ways. Some cases are:

The scammer learns information about a stolen or misplaced wallet.

Credit card information and personal data that are exposed during business data breaches.

Scammers who send convincing phishing emails and websites to get a person to provide their credit card information.

Scammers who place card skimmers in public places, such as at gas pumps and standalone ATMs, that record credit card numbers and pins.

Scammers with a skimming device that can record the information on a credit card's RFID chip if they're close enough.

A pre-authorized credit offer that is stolen from a letter box and used to apply for new and fraudulent credit cards.

**Type of identity theft #2:
Loan or rental fraud**

Loan or rental fraud is generally grouped into six categories:
Mortgage/Real Estate Loan

Apartment or house rentals

Auto Lending/Leasing

Business/Personal Loan

Federal Student Loan

Non-Federal Student Loan

Examples of identity theft with loans or rentals

Loan fraud occurs when information, facts, and figures are deliberately falsified in order to obtain a loan or rental. It can happen in both personal and business contexts. For example, the FBI defines mortgage fraud as any type of "material misstatement, misrepresentation, or omission relating to the property or potential mortgage relied upon by an insurer or lender to finance, purchase, or secure a loan."

To cite one case, in Sacramento, California, seven people were convicted of a $10 million mortgage scam in early 2019. To obtain mortgages, employees filled out applications with false information about customers' income, profession and savings. The company also sometimes used ghost buyers, which are a type of synthetic identity theft, when the credit scores of the real borrowers were too low, resulting in a $4 million loss for lenders.

Type of Identity Theft #3:
Phone or utility fraud

In 2019, all forms of identity theft related to telephone or utility fraud increased compared to the previous year. This includes the following categories:

Existing landline phone accounts

New landline phone accounts

Existing mobile phone accounts

New mobile phone accounts

Existing accounts for utilities

New Utility Accounts

Scammers know that there is a high demand for phone and utility services. These are services that practically everyone requires. It's easy prey for those looking to take advantage of customers trying to save on their bills.

How does phone and utility fraud happen?

There are two common types of phone and utility scams. The first is a phone call from a fake representative of a telephone service or utility company. The second is someone who goes to a person's own home with a scam related to promotional prices or products.

As for the phone call strategy, scammers tend to call and demand payment immediately in an aggressive manner. They may say that a person is behind on payments and threaten to block access to the service within a day if payment is not made.

In the door-to-door strategy, they will pose as legitimate sales representatives of those they visit at home. A red flag is that they offer much lower rates than what is currently paid. The goal is for the consumer to reveal personal data, such as their credit card number, bank account information, or social security number.

While those two cases greatly affect consumers, today companies have to deal with their own synthetic identity phone fraud and

DeepFace. Criminals recently used AI-based software to impersonate the voice of a CEO and demand a fraudulent transfer: an employee of an energy company thought he was on the phone with his boss, who asked him to send more than €200,000 to a Hungarian supplier. As a result, the funds were transferred and subsequently lost.

Today's digital identity can create profiles called "synthetic identities" with images that look like real people but are completely fake.

Balance the physical and digital worlds, have users use a real-world ID, and compare information and images with information from a form and a selfie photo provided by the user.

Monitor your credit score by receiving a credit report to stay on top of any new accounts that have been opened.

Enterprise identity verification: key to preventing identity theft.

In 2024, consumers are doing more than just doing a security freeze or sending a report alert to the lender when they discover that a breach of their personal information has occurred. With the rise of fake profiles in the virtual world, such as synthetic identities, or with increased adoption of fraud prevention products such as child identity theft protection, consumers are increasingly demanding that governments and businesses alike adopt security measures that limit the number of stolen identities and the damage done to their livelihoods. One solution that companies are adopting. Business identity verification.

Identity verification is a key factor in helping organizations prevent identity theft of their customers. As consumers are fully aware of the consequences of recent data breaches, with identity fraud cases on the rise, businesses are implementing identity verification into the onboarding process that protects their users from sensitive information breaches by malicious actors gaining access to a platform, as well as increasing their guaranteed rates knowing that they have incorporated more legal people and limiting abandonment rates.

How does digital identity verification work?

Hundreds of AI-based analytics and facial comparison algorithms work together to verify that a user is indeed the owner of a supplied ID document, to enable secure customer acquisition and the rapid movement of money, as well as prevent account takeover fraud.

ID document verification and facial biometrics work together to verify users' identities and provide a secure and convenient onboarding process, as well as an overall secure platform.

Identity theft is one of the fastest-growing crimes. It can take place at any time, and anyone is susceptible to being a victim, regardless of age. The best line of defense is arguably education and awareness, as well as ensuring that both government entities, public institutions and companies in general care about the safety, security and minimization of fraud with any means necessary.

Current Identity Theft Cases

In recent years, identity theft cases have evolved and diversified, affecting millions of people both digitally and in the real world. Below is a summary of some of the most recent and high-profile cases, with a particular focus on the United States and the steps the United States is taking to protect its citizens.

Case 1: Facebook (2019)

The case that I raise in the book is of vital importance today, the victim of this case was initially approached through a nascent social network that has become a real danger for unwary users who are unaware of the reach of criminal mafias.

Who stole my identity?

In 2019, data from more than 530 million Facebook users was found to be available online. This information included full names, phone numbers, email addresses, and locations. Although Facebook claimed that the

breach occurred before 2018, the impact on users' privacy was significant, highlighting the need to protect personal information on social networks. Facebook possesses an impressive amount of private information that can be used to steal your identity.

Identity theft protection is a must for all smartphone, tablet, and computer users that extends to social media, such as Facebook, Instagram, Twitter/X, etc. Due to the nature of social networking sites (where people are encouraged to share personal information), users are automatically at risk of becoming victims of identity theft.

Facebook users should be aware that identity thieves are constantly inventing new scams to steal personal data. And often, that data is publicly accessible and at your fingertips.

Here are some tips for protecting against identity theft and protecting your Facebook profile:
Don't post your date of birth, or at least don't post the year you were born. It may seem like a tactic for people who want to hold on to their youth for as long as possible, but in reality, it has a practical use: date of birth, including year, is a key piece of information for stealing your identity.
Think twice when you want to purchase Facebook services that require your credit card information. It's best to avoid putting that data on the site.

Have limits. Avoid revealing where a photo was taken and stop photo geotagging that shows the exact locations. Be cautious about posting photos that reveal your address or show where you keep valuables at home.

The more you publicly reveal where you are and what you're doing, identity thieves will no doubt notice. Delete photos and posts on the timeline that display personally identifiable information.

Your name, profile picture, and cover photo are always "public" and that cannot be changed. From this public information, thieves can create identical Facebook profiles with the intention of infecting users' devices with spyware that can steal valuable data. Use reputable internet security software on your device to rule out dangerous threats and achieve effective protection against identity theft. Also, be careful not to download free anti-spyware packages, as they could be cloaked malware.

Although in 2012, the Federal Trade Commission (FTC) reached an agreement with Facebook to ensure that the site took some privacy measures; It was good news for privacy-conscious users, the system was breached, so remember that you must be your own defender to prevent identity theft.

For more than a billion people (and counting), Facebook has been a place to connect with old friends, stay in touch across long distances, and promote new business ventures. If you use it wisely and with a little caution, Facebook can be a great tool. If not, the bad guys can ruin the fun.

Case 2: Equifax (2017)

One of the largest data breaches in history affected the credit bureau

Equifax, compromising the personal information of 147 million people. The hackers accessed names, Social Security numbers, dates of birth, addresses, and, in some cases, driver's license and credit card numbers. This incident underscored the importance of cybersecurity in institutions that handle sensitive data.

Case 3: Banco de Chile (2018)

Banco de Chile suffered a cyberattack that resulted in the theft of 10 million dollars. The attackers used malware to compromise the bank's systems and redirect the money to accounts in Hong Kong. This case showed how cybercriminals can orchestrate complex and well-coordinated attacks to steal large sums of money from financial institutions.

Case 4: SIM Swapping

SIM swapping has become a popular tactic among identity thieves. It involves convincing mobile phone companies to transfer a victim's phone number to a SIM card controlled by the attacker. This allows criminals to access bank accounts and social media profiles. Several high-profile cases, including that of Twitter CEO Jack Dorsey, have demonstrated the effectiveness and danger of this technique.

Case 5: Attacks on cryptocurrency platforms

Identity thefts in the crypto arena have increased, with notable cases such as Japanese platform Coincheck, which lost $530 million in crypto due to a hack. Not only do these attacks result in massive financial losses, but they also breed distrust in digital platforms.

Identity Theft in the United States and Protective Measures
Identity theft is a serious problem in the United States, affecting millions of citizens each year. In 2020, the Federal Trade Commission (FTC) received nearly 1.4 million reports of identity theft, a significant increase compared to previous years. The most common types include fraud related to government benefits, credit card fraud, and loan and lease fraud.

Protection Measures

To combat identity theft, the United States has implemented several measures and policies:

Legislation:

Identity Theft and Assumption Deterrence Act (1998): Establishes identity theft as a federal crime and provides legal tools to prosecute the culprits.
Fair and Accurate Credit Transactions Act (2003): Allows consumers to obtain a free credit report each year from the three major credit bureaus and set fraud alerts.
Gramm-Leach-Bliley Act (1999): Requires financial institutions to explain their information-sharing practices and protect their customers' confidential information.

Protection Agencies and Programs:

Federal Trade Commission (FTC): Leads the fight against identity theft by educating consumers and receiving fraud complaints. The FTC runs the IdentityTheft.gov site, where victims can report identity theft and get a personalized recovery plan.
Identity Theft Resource Center (ITRC): Offers free assistance to victims of identity theft, providing resources and support to recover their identity.

Technology and Security:

Multi-factor authentication (MFA): Implementing MFA has become crucial to securing online accounts, requiring users to verify their identity through multiple methods.

Encryption and Monitoring: Businesses and financial institutions are adopting advanced encryption practices and continuous monitoring to detect and prevent unauthorized access to sensitive data.

Education and Awareness:

Public education campaigns seek to inform citizens about how to protect their personal information and recognize the signs of identity theft. Government entities and non-profit organizations work to raise awareness of this issue.

The Danger of New Technologies and Artificial Intelligence Identity Theft

With the advancement of technologies, identity theft has taken on new forms, especially with the integration of artificial intelligence (AI). AI can be a powerful tool for criminals, enabling the creation of fake identities and spoofing with a high degree of accuracy.

Deepface

Deep Faces are an AI-based technology that allows you to create extremely realistic fake videos and audios. Criminals can use DeepFace to impersonate a person, carrying out fraud or deception that is difficult to detect.

DeepFace is a deep-learning facial recognition system created by a Facebook research group. Identify human faces in digital images. The program uses a nine-layer neural network with more than 120 million pesos of connection and was trained on four million images uploaded by Facebook users. The Facebook Research team has stated that the DeepFace method achieves an accuracy of 97.35% ±0.25% in the Tagged

Faces in the Wild (LFW) dataset, where humans have 97.53%. This means that DeepFace is sometimes more successful than humans. As a result of growing social concern, Meta announced that it plans to shut down Facebook's facial recognition system, deleting facial scan data from more than a billion users. This change will represent one of the biggest changes in the use of facial recognition in the history of technology. Facebook planned to remove more than a billion facial recognition templates, which are digital scans of facial features, by December 2021. However, it did not plan to remove DeepFace, which is the software that powers the facial recognition system. The company has also not ruled out incorporating facial recognition technology into future products, according to the Meta spokesperson.

Origin and Commercial Deployment

DeepFace was produced by a group of scientists from Facebook's AI research team. The team includes Yainiv Taigman and a Facebook research scientist, Ming Yang. They were also joined by Lior Wolf, a faculty member at Tel Aviv University. Yaniv Taigman came to Facebook when Facebook acquired Face.com in 2012.

Facebook began rolling out DeepFace to its users in early 2015 and has continually expanded the use and software of DeepFace, according to Facebook's director of AI research, it doesn't intend to invade individual privacy. Instead, DeepFace alerts people when their face appears in any photo posted on Facebook. When they receive this notification, they have the option to remove their face from the photo.

European Union

When DeepFace technology was initially implemented, users had the option to disable DeepFace. However, they were not notified that it was on. Because of this, DeepFace was not launched in the European Union. A data privacy law in the EU argued that Facebook's facial recognition did not comply with EU data protection laws. Because users do not consent to all uses of their biometric data, it does not comply.

Accuracy

DeepFace systems can identify faces with 97% accuracy, almost the same accuracy as a human in the same position. Facebook's facial recognition is more effective than the FBI's technology, which is 85% accurate. Google's technology, FaceNet, is more successful than DeepFace using the same datasets. FaceNet set a record for accuracy, 99.63%. Google's FaceNet incorporates data from Google Photos.

Applications

Facebook uses individual facial recognition templates to find photos in which a person appears so they can review, interact with, or share the content. DeepFace protects people from identity theft or identity theft.

Take, for example, a case where a person used someone's profile picture as their own. Through DeepFace, Facebook can identify and alert the person whose information is being misused. To ensure that people have control over their facial recognition, Facebook does not share facial templates. In addition, Facebook will remove images from facial recognition templates if someone has deleted their account or untagged themselves from a photo. People have the option to turn off facial recognition on Facebook. If the feature is disabled, Facebook will no longer recognize that person's face.

DeepFace was launched in 2015, but its use has remained relatively stagnant. Because more people have uploaded images to Facebook, the algorithm has become more accurate. Facebook's DeepFace is the largest facial recognition dataset currently in existence. Because of this, some people argue that Facebook's facial ID database could be distributed to government agencies. These uses, however, would be prohibited by most data privacy laws. In response to privacy concerns, Facebook removed its automatic facial recognition feature, allowing people to opt out of tagging through DeepFace. This change was implemented in 2019.

Reactions to DeepFace

Industry

AI researcher Ben Goertzel said Facebook had "pretty convincingly solved facial recognition" with the project but said it would be incorrect to conclude that deep learning is the complete solution for AI.
Neeraj Kumar, a researcher at the University of Washington, said Facebook's DeepFace shows how large external data sets can result in a

"higher capacity" model. Because of Facebook's extensive access to images of individuals, its facial recognition software may perform better than other software with much smaller datasets.

Media

A Huffington Post article called the technology "creepy," citing concerns about data privacy, noting that some European governments had already required Facebook to remove facial recognition data. According to Broadcasting & Cable, both Facebook and Google had been invited by the Center for Digital Democracy to attend a National Telecommunications and Information Administration "stakeholder meeting" in 2014 to help develop a Consumer Privacy Bill of Rights, but both declined. Broadcasting & Cable also noted that Facebook had not published any press announcements about DeepFace, although its investigative paper had been published earlier in the month. Slate said Facebook wasn't advertising DeepFace because it's wary of another round of headlines denouncing DeepFace's creepy.

Users

Many people fear facial recognition technology. "The technology's near-perfect accuracy allows social media companies to create digital profiles of millions of Americans." ("DeepFace - Wikipedia") However, an individual's fear of facial recognition and other privacy concerns does not correspond with a decline in social media use. Instead, attitudes toward privacy and privacy settings don't have a huge impact on an individual's intent to use Facebook apps. Because Facebook is a social networking site, individual fears about privacy are overridden by a desire to engage in social media.

DeepFace Privacy Issues / Bipa Lawsuit

Facebook users filed a class-action lawsuit against Facebook under the Illinois Biometric Information Privacy Act (BIPA). Illinois has the most comprehensive biometric privacy legislation, which regulates the collection of biometric information by business entities. The Illinois BIPA requires a corporation that obtains a person's biometric information to obtain a written release, provide them with notice that their information is being collected, and state the duration of the information to be collected. The lawsuit filed against DeepFace alleges that Facebook's collection of facial identification information for the purpose of the tag suggestion tool violates BIPA. Because Facebook does not give notice or consent to people when they use this tool, Facebook users argue that it violates BIPA. The Ninth Circuit denied Facebook's motion to dismiss the case and ultimately certified the case. Facebook attempted to appeal the certification of the Ninth Circuit's decision that was ultimately granted. Facebook claims that the case should not have been verified because the plaintiffs have not alleged any harm beyond Facebook's violation of BIPA. Facebook removed its automatic facial recognition labeling feature in 2019, in response to concerns raised in the lawsuit. Facebook proposed a $550 million settlement for the case, which was rejected. When Facebook increased the settlement to $650 million, the court accepted it. In early March 2021, Facebook was ordered to pay its $650 million settlement. 1.6 million Illinois residents will receive at least $345.

In July 2020, Facebook announced that it is building teams that will investigate racism in its algorithms. Facebook teams will work with Facebook's responsible AI team to study bias in their systems. The implementation of these programs is recent, and it is not yet clear what reforms will be made.

Ten-year challenge

In 2019, a Facebook challenge went viral asking users to post a photo from 10 years ago and one from 2019. The challenge was coined the "10-year challenge." More than 5 million people participated in the challenge, including many celebrities. Concerns arose that Facebook's 10-year challenge was designed to train Facebook's facial recognition database. Kate O'Neill, a writer for Wired, wrote an op-ed that echoed this possibility. Facebook denied that they played a role in generating the challenge. However, people have argued that the concerns underscored by theories around the 10-year challenge echo broader concerns about Facebook and the right to privacy.

Racism in Facial ID Technology

Facial recognition algorithms are not universally successful. While the algorithms are capable of classifying faces with more than 90% accuracy in some cases, the accuracy is lower when the algorithms are sent to women, black individuals, and young people. The systems falsely identify black and Asian faces 10 to 100 times more than white faces. Because algorithms are primarily trained on white men, systems like DeepFace have a harder time identifying them. It is projected that once facial recognition databases are trained to identify people of color — exposing them to more diverse faces — they will be more successful at identification.

Chatbots and automated fraud

AI chatbots can be programmed to perform large-scale phishing attacks, interacting with victims in real-time to extract personal and financial information. These bots can convincingly mimic representatives of companies or institutions, causing victims to trust them and provide sensitive data.

Voice Theft

Voice cloning technology uses AI to replicate a person's voice from audio samples. Criminals can use these mirrors to make fraudulent calls, trick family, friends, or institutions into obtaining personal information, or make financial transactions.

AI spoofing protection measures that should be implemented.

To combat these new threats, specific measures are crucial:

Detection Technologies:

Anti-deepfake software: Advanced tools that detect manipulation in videos and audios, alerting users to possible fraud.

Biometric verification systems: Use multiple biometric factors, such as facial, voice, and behavioral recognition, to authenticate user identities.

Rules and Regulations:

Malicious Use of AI Laws: Implement legislation that criminalizes the use of AI technologies to commit fraud and phishing.

AI Safety Standards: Establish standards and guidelines for the development and safe use of AI technologies.

Education and Awareness:

Information campaigns: Informing the public about the risks associated with new technologies and how to identify potential fraud.

Cybersecurity training: Train employees and users on best practices to protect against phishing and malicious use of AI.

These combined efforts seek to reduce the incidence of identity theft and mitigate its effects, protecting citizens and strengthening the security of personal information in the United States and why not in the world.

In conclusion, all this material that I deliver thanks to my research team and advisors is in order to alert thousands of people who may be victims of identity theft, like the young man who personifies my story. We must protect ourselves personally, there is no other alternative.

I hope that this material has been helpful and useful and that you share it with your loved ones, who will thank you.

"I would, if I could, trade all my technology for an afternoon with Socrates."

Steve Jobs

ABOUT THE AUTHOR

Ángel Martínez
A Passionate Researcher, Writer and Lecturer.

Angel Martinez is an international private investigator with extensive experience. A renowned communicator and lecturer, who has also dedicated himself in recent years to the training of new generations of researchers and to capturing their experiences in captivating stories.

Angel Martinez, born in Santiago, Dominican Republic, is the younger of two children of Christian parents. His first steps in espionage were taken as a child when American troops, on April 24, 1965, invaded his country.

After his primary studies he entered the seminary to study priesthood, most of his youth was dedicated to evangelizing and educating young people against drug use, he is a foreign correspondent for some newspapers and television channels.

He currently has more than one million followers on social media and is a regular guest on social media in the Dominican Republic, Honduras, and the United States.

Seeking the American dream, he immigrated to the United States more than 50 years ago, first working for a law firm, the latter brought him closer to Federal agencies, for which he worked under the supervision of excellent American agents.

He served in the FBI, Immigration, Secret Service, DEA, Customs, New York Police and other intelligence institutions.

He has testified in Federal and State courts on behalf of the United States against organizations related to drug trafficking. In the performance of his duties, he has traveled around the world in covert operations.

His innumerable investigations against drug trafficking have qualified him as an expert on the subject.

He has given lectures on drug trafficking in the main universities of Latin America, as well as in various Book Fairs, Schools, Prisons, Clubs and private institutions. Today, the main newspapers in Latin America and the United States have echoed his statements in large front-page headlines.

He has been kidnapped three times, emerging victorious thanks to the spectacular rescue work of the Delta Counterintelligence Force.

His best years have been dedicated to fighting drug trafficking, demonstrating that the solution to the problem lies in consumption and not in the drug trafficker. A successful author with relevant topics.

His works, acclaimed by his followers, address crucial and current issues such as drug trafficking, organized crime and identity theft, connecting with an audience eager for true stories and with a powerful message.

Reference works:

After years of experience and research, Ángel Martínez has compiled his knowledge in the "International Detective's Manual", a work that has become a reference for professionals in private investigation. This practical guide, full of theory and real cases, is indispensable for any researcher who aspires to excellence.

A cry against injustice: "La Cocaína al desnudo", his most powerful work, is a forceful denunciation of the trafficking and consumption of cocaine in the United States, and the struggle of the indigenous peoples who produce and consume the coca leaf. A story that does not leave indifferent and that seeks to raise awareness about this scourge that affects thousands.

True stories that captivate:

All of Ángel Martínez's novels bear the stamp of drama that only reality can offer. His agile and close narrative style makes his stories easy to read, catching the reader from the first page.

A commitment to society:

Its main objective is to raise awareness among the world's population about drug abuse and illicit trafficking, two serious problems that plague society, especially young people.

A highly topical topic:

In its second edition, "Who Stole My Identity?" offers, in the context of a true story, a call to attention to how we are exposed to identity theft by criminal mafias. A more than current issue in the digital age, where personal information is at constant risk.

Expanding your reach:
In this new stage of 2024, Ángel Martínez's main works, "La cocaína al desnudo", "¿Quién se robó mi identidad?" and "La Mujer del Sicario", will be translated into English, taking his message to an even wider audience and consolidating his position as an author of international stature.

Ángel Martínez: A researcher, writer and lecturer who not only tells stories, but lives them. A professional committed to truth and justice, who uses his pen as a tool to fight against the scourges that afflict society.

All the profits generated by his books and conferences have been donated to institutions that fight to give a better life to drug users.

All the works of Ángel Martínez can be found in:

www.angelmartinezescritor.com

RESOURCES USED

Links are in Spanish original resources.

Wikipedia: https://es.wikipedia.org/wiki/Robo_de_identidad

Federal Government Commission, USA:
https://www.robodeidentidad.gov/

Mcafee: What Is Identity Theft and How to Recover from It?
https://www.mcafee.com/learn/es-mx/que-es-el-robo-de-identidad-y-como-recuperarse-de-el/

Federal Government Commission, USA, How to avoid identity theft?
https://consumidor.gov/estafas-y-el-robo-de-identidad/evitar-el-robo-de-identidad

CONTENT